To Sharon, with love and gratitude

Think
Straight!
Feel
Great!
21 Guides to Emotional Self-Control

Bill Borcherdt, ACSW

Professional Resource Exchange, Inc.
Sarasota, Florida

Printed in the United States of America

Paperbound Edition ISBN: 0-943158-53-2
Library of Congress Catalog Number: 88-43055

The copy editors for this book were Janet Sailian and Barbara Robarge, the typist was Marydale Rogan, the production supervisor was Debbie Fink, the graphics coordinator was Judy Warinner, and the cover designer was Bill Tabler.

About the Author

Bill Borcherdt, ACSW, Diplomate in Clinical Social Work, has been a psychotherapist for 21 years. He has counseled individuals, couples, parents, families, and groups with varying emotional and relationship problems. He received his masters degree in social work from the University of Wisconsin-Milwaukee in 1967. From 1967-1970 he was a social work officer in the United States Army Medical Service Corps. Since 1970 he has been a full-time social work therapist at the Winnebago County Mental Health Clinic in Neenah, Wisconsin, and has his own private practice. For the past 12 years, he has taught graduate and undergraduate courses, as well as continuing education programs at both state and national levels. He is well-known for his informative and witty presentations. Bill has completed the Associate Fellowship and Supervision of Rational-Emotive Therapy training programs at the Institute for Rational-Emotive Therapy in New York City. He lives in Menasha, Wisconsin, with his wife Sharon and their two children.

Bill is available for mental health presentations and training workshops on the various topics of rational living as reflected in his writings. He may be contacted at 1217 Deerfield Avenue, Menasha, WI 54952.

Table of Contents

good

Introduction

This book contains 21 guides for dealing with common problems in living. Each articulates Rational-Emotive Therapy (RET) principles. Originally written as adjunctive resources for use by psychotherapists in work with clients, they may also be used by individuals who are exploring options for personal growth.

Rational-Emotive Therapy is a philosophical, educational, and therapeutic approach developed by psychologist Albert Ellis. Dr. Ellis is currently director of the Institute for Rational-Emotive Therapy and the Institute for Rational Living in New York City. He and his colleagues have developed numerous books and other resources that are listed in a catalog available from The Institute for Rational-Emotive Therapy, 45 East 65th Street, New York, NY 10021.

RET teaches people how to get along better with themselves and others by disciplining their thinking, emotions, and behaviors. In the context of RET, rational living means developing thoughts, feelings, and behaviors that abet one's happiness and survival. RET encourages people to assume responsibility for their own lives in an action-oriented, spirited, and adventuresome manner - to go out on the limb where the fruit is; to plant their own garden rather than wait for someone to bring them flowers.

RET is applied philosophy. It focuses on new ways of looking at old problems. RET teaches that anything that is believed can be disbelieved. It questions much of conventional wisdom, while encouraging participants to see that there are many ways to look at life. RET avoids orthodox ways of thinking, while clearly distinguishing what is "normal" from what is "healthy."

RET is humanistic in that it doesn't presume the inevitability of emotional disturbance following unfortunate events. It insists that circumstances, no matter how difficult, need not create emotional disturbance. In RET theory, emotional disturbance is philosophically based and represents a protest against reality, a refusal to accept what exists. By accepting what exists and thinking differently about this reality, one can overcome emotional disturbance. Individuals can achieve emotional health by learning to think in ways that help them feel more the way they want to feel and less the way they don't want to feel. RET disputes the unprovable ways of thinking that invite emotional upset. It encourages verifiable, scientific thinking, which allows for more personal happiness.

One of RET's unique perspectives is that it encourages problem-solving on philosophical grounds first, and on practical foundations second. Individuals are urged to deal with their inner conflicts before working on external difficulties. This orientation encourages thinking that not only helps with immediate problems but develops personal resources for dealing with those problematic situations that will arise throughout one's life. In this way, RET allows for gains within gains, permitting people to become more tolerant and self-accepting.

RET is not just a set of pragmatic, expedient, skill-training procedures. RET teaches individuals how to change the ways in which they view themselves and others; it teaches efficient means of coping with life's problems without creating secondary problems in the form of guilt, shame, self-blame, and low frustration tolerance. By dealing with these secondary problems first, it stresses that as long as people upset themselves about having problems, they will not be able to work effectively to get through the problems. The guides within this book are based on a number of powerful RET principles. These principles are:

1. *Teaching That Feelings Are Not Externally Caused.* Although people experience feelings in particular circumstances, those circumstances do not cause the feelings. Instead, a person's emotional response reflects his or her thinking about the circumstances. People feel not so much in response to what happens to them, but in response to what they think about what happens. This is a major revelation, because people have control over what they think, even when they can't control what happens. By controlling their thoughts, individuals can gain emotional self-control. Happenings don't cause feelings; happenings plus thoughts do.

2. *Recognizing That Dissatisfaction Is Different from, and Does Not Inevitably Lead to, Disturbance.* People and circumstances can frustrate, deprive, and inconvenience you, but only you can disturb yourself. You create disturbances for yourself by insisting that dissatisfactions should not exist.

3. *Recognizing That All Rejection Is Self-Rejection and Is Self-Inflicted.* People can select and discriminate against your traits and features that displease them, but only you can reject yourself by thinking: "Because so and so doesn't like me, I'm no damn good."

4. *Acknowledging Preference Versus Demand As the Dividing Line Between Sanity and Disturbance.* Society and individuals have standards of what they regard as desirable, that is, to succeed,

achieve, perform well, or be liked and accepted. It is only when the individual escalates these preferences into demands ("I have to have what I find desirable") that disturbance erupts. RET emphasizes the value of being preferentially motivated and the emotional hazard of being demandingly insistent.

5. *Abolishing Illusory Human Needs.* RET teaches that nothing in life "has to be." You don't even have to survive; you choose to survive because you want to survive. Arbitrarily defining wants as needs creates a sense of urgency and desperation, emotionally blocking goal direction and self-control.

6. *Distinguishing Appropriate Feelings from Inappropriate Feelings.* Feelings that are against your best interests are inappropriate. These include anger, guilt, anxiety, and depression. Appropriate feelings include annoyance, regret, apprehension, and sadness.

7. *Unashamedly Valuing Self-Interest.* Putting yourself first and others a close second promotes happiness and joy, and makes you more loving and fun to be around.

8. *Avoiding Evaluation of Humans.* RET emphasizes the unratability of human beings. Humans are too complex and ever-changing to score by some arbitrary standard, and to try only promotes unhappiness and misery.

9. *Doing the Right Thing for the Right Reason.* You can put life's goals and accomplishments in better perspective by seeking what you value for practical, happiness-giving reasons rather than for ego or approval-seeking reasons.

10. *Avoiding Overemphasis on Change.* Humans are remarkably fallible, and can learn to co-exist peacefully with their problems and imperfections rather than putting undue pressure on themselves to overcome all problems.

11. *Attempting to Get Better, Not Merely Feel Better.* To unreflectively express unwanted feelings (such as anger) can result in feeling better but getting worse. Practicing expression of unde-

sirable emotions may feel good but not actually be good for you. RET tries to get at the philosophical notions that create the emotions so individuals can learn to control them before they build up.

12. *Abandoning Absolutist Thinking.* RET tries to identify, challenge, and uproot these three core irrational ideas:

- "I must do perfectly well (or else I'm perfectly worthless)." This idea causes depression or guilt in the face of failure, and anxiety in the throes of success, due to the demand for continued success. It can be disputed with: "Why do I have to prove that I'm superhuman, and where is the evidence that I am diminished as a human being when I falter?"
- "You must do well by me and treat me with no lapses in kindness and consideration (or else you're equally worthless)." This idea creates feelings of anger, resentment, and fury. It can be debated with: "Where is the proof that others are required to do well by me? Don't they have a right to be wrong, even when it means wronging me?"
- "Life must make it easy on me to reach my goals to achieve my ends (or else it's unbearably worthless)." This idea generates undisciplined whining, listlessness, and self-pity. It can best be argued against with: "Where can it be verified that life was designed to be hassle-free, and what good does it do to moan and groan when I don't get my piece of taffy as easily as I would like?"

RET intervenes in human thought in unique ways. Its disputational methods and refreshing world view permit a loosening of frozen judgments. When people unshackle themselves from living by rigid rules, they become more emotionally flexible and clearheaded in approaching life circumstances. RET discourages choice-blocking emotions that work against happiness and survival interests and encourages people to freely choose those feelings that contribute to a more fully enjoyable life.

Mental health is not the absence of problems. It is knowing what to realistically expect of yourself, of others, and of life. In determining quality of emotional life, there is a direct ratio between what people expect and what they get. Unfortunately, what most people expect of themselves is perfection; what they get is fallibility. What they frequently expect from others is kind, pleasant treatment; what they often get is ordinary or normal neglect. What is sought from life is fairness and justice; what can be gained is objectivity and impartiality. Perhaps the one word that best describes mental health is "acceptance" - undamning acceptance of self, others, and life. The cartoon character Ziggy put it differently: "My problem is that I like things as they aren't." RET aims for undamning acceptance. This approach doesn't hit the bulls-eye every time, but by taking center aim, it is likely to be on target more often than less elegant approaches to living.

I have used the Rational-Emotive guides in this book as supplemental reading in my work with clients and students, many of whom struggled with liking things as they aren't. Each guide contains a number of central rational ideas that can be generalized and applied to numerous difficult circumstances. One quickly discovers that RET principles do not merely provide "band-aid" assistance for specific difficulties, but instead offer "major surgery" through new ways of clear thinking and problem-solving in all areas of living.

Think Straight! Feel Great!

21 Guides to Emotional Self-Control

To Feel or Not to Feel - That Is <u>Not</u> the Question: Values and Mental Health

Principles of rational thinking are sometimes criticized as mechanical, hard-shelled, or otherwise unfeeling. This is far from the truth for at least two reasons:

1. A central goal of rational thinking as taught in Rational-Emotive Therapy (RET) is to free people from their choice-blocking, unhealthy feelings of anger, depression, anxiety, fear, guilt, and shame, so that they can freely choose to create more feelings of happiness and joy - to experience more wholesome aliveness and less discouragement or hopelessness.

2. Rational thinking makes the distinction between appropriate feelings, those that are in one's best interests, and inappropriate feelings, those that are against one's best interests. By teaching and encouraging more of the former and less of the latter, rational thinking aspires to bring about hope for gaining more of the delight and less of the exhaustion that life has to offer. Rather than stifle feelings, rational thinking makes it more convenient to experience feelings abundantly, in a fully humanistic way!

1

This guide provides an understanding of how both self-serving and self-defeating emotions are created, demonstrating that emotional expression is a choice. It shows how rational thinking deals with the core values and philosophies that provide existential meaning to life. Four sets of appropriate and inappropriate feelings, along with the cognitive or belief system correlates that produce them, will be examined.

1. *Sadness Versus Depression.* Sadness contributes to happiness and survival because it allows you to acknowledge disappointment which, in turn, will promote incentive to change those things that bring displeasure. Amplify the sadness and you have depression, which will deflate motivation and narrow your vision so that you see only blue. You are more likely to give up in the face of "hopeless" adversity. Depression, like practically all emotional disturbance, begins with frustration - a wish, want, desire, or preference that gets blocked or thwarted.

For example, if something doesn't go right, or somebody doesn't act your way, demandingness and self-blaming may follow disappointment and sadness. Thinking, "I wish this wasn't happening"; or "I would prefer and find it highly desirable that matters be different, but I'm not a bad person because of my bad situation," will create a healthy sense of sadness. This appropriate state of mind is clearly distinguished from the depression that comes from self-stating, "I must have matters and people in my favor, and I'm a bad person for not being able to make this happen."

Escalating desires, preferences, and wishes into demands and then blaming oneself for not being able to attain them triggers depression. Stick with highly preferring what you value, and you will remain alert and in sync with your life's ambitions. Then, if you fall short of the mark in realizing your values, you will be more likely to continue progressing towards

2

those goals. There is an emotional difference between telling yourself "I have to do well, and I'm a real numskull when I don't"; and "It would be delightful to achieve my aims, but I do not rate as a worthless, sinister slob if I don't hit the bulls-eye!"

2. *Annoyance and Irritation Versus Anger.* Annoyance and irritation are protective emotions. If you didn't feel them, you probably wouldn't care much how others treated or mistreated you. Without this sense of guardedness in the face of others' ill-advised treatment, you might lay down and emotionally die while permitting yourself to be used. Annoyance mobilizes self-protection by either creating a temporary distance between you and your adversary or forthrightly establishing boundaries on how much guff you're willing to take.

Anger, on the other hand, goes beyond protection and limit-setting to destruction and revenge. With depression, most of what you see is blue; with anger you see red. In either case, the result is the same - tunnel thinking with mostly self-defeating alternatives. With depression you get down on yourself; with anger you get down on others - each in its own way defeating the rational purposes of life: to live, survive, and be happy.

Anger, too, begins with a sense of dissatisfaction. Someone doesn't do something that you would have liked or does something that you would have liked them not to do, and your reaction, "I would just as soon . . ." or "I would rather you not act in certain ways," is carried to demanding and blaming proportions. Instead of patience, it's, "Patience nothing, I'm going to kill somebody!" Calling to mind the idea, "I very much hope that my associate would act and think in more kindly and highly efficient ways, and it sure is disappointing and decidedly frustrating when he exercises his prerogative and doesn't," will permit you to feel

3

sanely irritated and to express grievances in a civilized manner.

Contrast that with the more intolerant perspective, "Because I strongly want my friend to extend himself beyond his attitudinal limits in a way that I know is best for him, he absolutely *has* to follow suit with my way of thinking, and if he doesn't he deserves to be condemned and to roast to a frazzle in Haiti to learn what is best." Such unrealistic demands, coupled with the condemnation of others for not complying, leads to anger, hatred, and bitterness.

By convincing yourself that as wrong as people might be, they nevertheless have the right to be wrong, you will take a giant step forward in unharnessing yourself from hostile feelings that put you at odds with yourself and others. Simply replacing "he should," or "he has to," with "I would like him to," or "it would be nice (but hardly necessary)," will help you maintain a boundary between reasonable frustration and unreasonable anger.

3. *Apprehension and Concern Versus Fear and Anxiety.* A healthy sense of apprehension or concern keeps you on your toes, allowing keener preparation for what lies ahead. By contrast, an unhealthy portion of fear or anxiety will likely knock you off your feet, so that you blunder through the upcoming task. Advantageous feelings of apprehension and concern are likely to be preceded by the self-sentence, "Wouldn't it be disappointing and unfortunate if matters did not turn out my way; if I failed, was rejected, or was injured?" By contrast, the following self-statements are likely to precede undue fear and anxiety: "Wouldn't it be an awful catastrophe if matters would not bend my way and it turned out I failed or was harmed in some way?" or, "Because it is possible that the worst could occur, I should keep brooding and dwelling on it, as if it were probable or even inevitable that this will happen."

This is how a keen, deliberate sense of possible disappointment balloons into an exasperated feeling of pending disaster.

Awareness of possible risks and dangers in upcoming activity better prepares you for these events, whereas absorption in anticipated calamity leaves you emotionally immersed in negative outcomes that may never occur. As Mark Twain once said, "My life has been full of devastation - most of which has never happened."

4. *Regret Versus Guilt.* Without a moderate degree of regret and sorrow for your mistakes and ill-advised actions that deprive, frustrate, and bring disadvantages to your social group, you would lapse into being an uncaring, casual, flippant-acting human being. Such "I couldn't care less," "I don't give a shit" attitudes would soon put you at odds with your associates. Realistically, it is best not to "bite the hands that feed you" if you wish to continue to eat.

Viewing others' inconveniences that are at least in part influenced by your behavior as unfortunate and preferably avoided will cultivate a self- and other-interested give-and-take with your peers. By contrast, guilt, with its dimensions of devastation and self-blame, adds fuel to the fire at a time when it is burning hot enough already. Thinking, "How regretful that I have acted in ways that have contributed to others' dissatisfactions," will likely provide the motivation to clean up your act and do better by your social companions next time around. Believing, "How terrible of me for being an obstacle to my colleague's happiness, and what a bad person I am for doing such a terrible act," will hold up the correcting process while you needlessly beat yourself over the head in self-defeating atonement for your poor judgment. Such an exaggerated view of consequences, and such penance-seeking, self-downing attitudes and activities may leave you too busy to correct your faults in the future. Guilt is like a traffic jam - it holds everything up. Regret is like a traffic director - it provides for alternative routes to follow the next time around.

HEALTHY AND UNHEALTHY
SELF-STATEMENTS

Next, let's review the four basic feelings and the thoughts that propel both self-defeating and self-fulfilling emotions. Below are lists of thoughts that contribute to each of the unhealthy feelings, followed by corrective thoughts that may lead to healthier emotional reactions.

THOUGHTS THAT LEAD
TO UNHEALTHY DEPRESSION

- "How stupid I am for acting stupidly."
- "Because I have no right to be so wrong, I rate as a bad, damnable person when I do act badly."
- "Life really owes me the things that I miss; it has no right to treat me unfairly; I feel awful when I come out on the short end of the stick - woe is me."
- "I can't stand conditions in my life - they stink."
- "I don't have a right to fail."
- "I have to be perfect or else I'm perfectly worthless."
- "I'm disappointed in me."
- "Damn me."

COUNTERING THOUGHTS THAT
INVITE HEALTHY SADNESS

- "Granted, I acted stupidly, but I'm not stupid."
- "Though I do have a right to be wrong, I'd best try not to be wrong as much as is humanly possible; but because I'm not the same as my behavior, I am not bad when I act badly."
- "It is certainly frustrating when conditions don't lean in my favor, but if I wait for life to do my work for me, I might have to wait until hell freezes over."

6

- "Matters in my life surely could be a lot more favorable, and perhaps some day they will be. In the meantime, I can tolerate what I don't like as long as I'm alive."
- "Because I am human, I have a right to fail."
- "I can lighten up, go easy, give myself some slack - doing my best doesn't mean doing *the* best."
- "I can acknowledge my mistakes and hold myself accountable - be disappointed in them but not in me."
- "I can correct my mistakes without condemning myself for making them."

THOUGHTS THAT LEAD
TO UNWANTED ANGER

- "He doesn't have a right to go against my values."
- "He has no right to treat me badly, and he rates as a bad, worthless person when he does."
- "I'll get even and hurt him back."
- "I hate him!"
- "I can't stand him when he doesn't see that I am right."
- "I have every right to get angry."

THOUGHTS THAT PROVIDE
BENEFICIAL IRRITATION

- "He has free will - not my will."
- "I wish he wouldn't exercise his right to treat me with lapses in kindness and consideration, and it is very frustrating when he does. However, no one in this life is required by universal law to cater to me in any manner, shape, or form."
- "It's impossible to hurt someone else without hurting yourself; bittersweet revenge, who needs it?"
- "I highly disapprove of if not despise his antics, but I don't have to condemn him for his negative behavior."
- "True, I don't like it when he goes against my way of thinking; untrue that he or everybody else must cater to my sacred opinions."

● "Correct, I have the right to get angry, but do I really want to do something that will probably hurt me, too?"

THOUGHTS THAT LEAD TO CHOICE-BLOCKING FEAR AND ANXIETY

● "How dreadful it would be to fail."
● "I have to get others to like me."
● "What if the worst should happen?"
● "Because this matter seems dangerous and fearsome, I should dwell on it and brood about the worst occurrence, so I will be better prepared for catastrophe."
● "Others' opinions of me equal me."
● "Others might reject me and that would be devastating.
● "I have to perform faster and better than anyone else."
● "The world would come to an end if _____ _____."
● "But I've been such a nervous person all my life."
● "Anxious people like myself are inferior beings."

THOUGHTS THAT ENCOURAGE KEEN APPREHENSION AND CONCERN

● "Failure is not my first choice, but it would be bearable and, if nothing else, possibly I would learn what wasn't for me. Why mountain climb over mole hills?"
● "I want others to think well of me, and I'm going to put my best foot forward to make it convenient for them to do so. If they don't, I will survive."
● "I'll face the worst if and when it happens, and cope the best I can."
● "The more I stew about possibilities, the more upset I'll get myself, making it more likely I'll clumsily create the conditions I don't want."
● "Others' opinions of me tell me about their tastes and preferences; they tell very little about me."

- "All rejection is self-rejection; none can reject me but me."
- "Slow down, go easy, cool it, lighten up."
- "Disadvantages may befall me if . . ., but it is highly unlikely that the world will stop spinning on its axis or the sun will burn out."
- "If I ate manure all my life, would I have to continue eating it? The past is a bridge to the present and doesn't determine the future."
- "Although anxiety is, for the most part, a negative characteristic, I have many other features, some good, some bad, none of which determines who I am. I can accept myself with my anxiety; now let me see what I can do to work against it."

THOUGHTS THAT LEAD
TO UNDESIRABLE GUILT

- "If I am guilty, I should feel guilty."
- "If I'm at fault, then I'm blameworthy."
- "If I don't make myself feel good and guilty, I won't try to do better."
- "I deserve to be punished."
- "I'm stupid for feeling guilty."
- "It's normal to feel guilty for making mistakes, so I should do what's normal."
- "If I don't feel guilty, I become an immoral, uncaring person."

THOUGHTS THAT PAVE THE
WAY TO CORRECTIVE REGRET

- "I best admit my wrongdoing so I can correct it. However, if I feel guilty, I'm likely to beat myself over the head about the problem rather than solve it."
- "I'm not required to, and I'd best not blame myself for my faults."
- "Self-correction, yes; self-condemnation, no!"
- "I deserve to be fair to myself regardless of my mistake."

9

- "Feeling guilty isn't the wisest thing to do, but I don't have to pass judgment on myself for my unwise behavior."
- "It's normal common practice to feel guilty after you goof, but normal doesn't mean healthy or better."
- "Nonsense! In fact, by not making myself feel guilty for using poor judgment, I'll become a freer-giving, caring person to those I care about or hope to care about."

Because you have feelings about practically everything you do in life, the value of reflectively sorting these experiences is extremely important. The principles of rational thinking encourage you to examine the distinctive thought processes that help you feel more the way you want to and less the way you don't want to. People largely create their own emotions, and by examining your thinking you can begin to make your feelings more appropriate and less distressing.

Human beings cannot turn their feelings off and on like hot and cold running water. However, they can learn to clarify their feelings - to distinguish between those that encourage a fuller appreciation of life and those that block such harmony. When you understand that you are creating and dealing with your own appropriate, self-interested feelings, you will also be less likely to create crises and consequently be in a better position to navigate through life's circumstances. Understanding yourself as not really depressed, guilty, fearful, or angry makes it much easier to approach problems deliberately and productively. Openly accepting feelings of sadness, regret, apprehension, or irritation helps stem emotional over-reaction. Sensitivity to your feelings through awareness of the thoughts that trigger them can be a preventive tool in avoiding unwanted emotional and behavioral results. Openly accepting and valuing appropriate feelings also confirms your mental health as value-oriented, while giving zest and incentive to life. At the same time, your efforts acknowledge that you value your living experience enough to vitally pursue what you believe is important.

Note. From *Think Straight! Feel Great! 21 Guides to Emotional Self-Control* by Bill Borcherdt, ACSW, Copyright 1989, Professional Resource Exchange, Inc., P.O. Box 15560, Sarasota, FL 34277-1560.

Eight Ways to Influence Someone Who Doesn't Want to Be Influenced

When you choose to remain in a relationship in which you seem to be consistently treated with sullenness, impatience, irritability, and moodiness - if not outright hostility, vengefulness, and negative criticism - what can be done to decrease such negative attitudes and actions? What can you do to more positively influence your associate while sensibly controlling your own response to such annoying habits, characteristics, and features?

You may have decided to remain in such a troubled arrangement for several reasons: (a) After having itemized and calculated the pros and cons - the pluses and the minuses of the overall relationship - you have decided that there are more of the former and less of the latter. (b) Because of financial or other practical reasons, it just would not be in your best interests to leave now. (c) You want to work on increasing your frustration tolerance by demonstrating to yourself that you can stand what you don't like. You might then be better able to increase your tolerance and acceptance level in other present and future relationships.

Although we can't determine how others behave and vice versa, we do influence one another; in some degree we can teach people how to respond to us by how we respond to them. This can be achieved in the following ways:

1. *Don't Blame Yourself.* Try not to internalize and personalize the other's problems and disturbances. For instance, if you are living with a difficult acting person, don't beat yourself over the head by assuming that you are responsible for his or her seemingly fixed state of upset. Telling yourself that you're not responsible for others' problems and disturbances does *not* mean you care about them less. To think otherwise will only lead to a problem about the problem in the form of guilt and depression.

2. *Don't Blame the Other Person.* Others' negative attributes reflect their own insecurity, telling you more about them than about you. Blaming them only reinforces their inclinations to get down on themselves and to take others too seriously. As self-blame will lead to depression, other-blame will create your own angry feelings, contributing further to the disruption of the relationship. Then two people will be upset, escalating the already high-pitched emotional climate. The longer you stay upset about others' problems, the longer it will take them to settle down. The less upset you get and the less you feed it, the sooner deliberation is likely to reign.

3. *Accept the Situation As Is.* Don't play "fairytale" by telling yourself these problems "shouldn't be." You don't have to like them, but you may as well accept them because they *do* exist. All emotional disturbance is a protest against reality; to deny what is by demanding that the situation be different will only cause secondary problems.

4. *Set Limits of Compromise/Conditions of the Relationship.* All relationships have conditions attached to them. No duo has as their everlasting motto, "What is mine is yours and what is

14

yours is mine." It is generally true that the fewer the conditions in a relationship, the smoother it will run because there will be fewer boundary disputes. However, even intimate lovers have conditions as part of their togetherness. Witness the couple who thought they subscribed fully to the "mutually unconditional" relationship model. One day, one partner had lost his toothbrush and asked the other if he could borrow hers. The telltale response was, "No, that is a condition of our relationship: You can't borrow my toothbrush."

How you say something is just as important as what you say. There is a difference between telling someone how you feel and telling them off. When defining a relationship expectation it can be helpful to (a) start out with a positive rather than a negative declaration, and (b) begin with an "I" rather than a "you" statement. Thus, in an effort to build bridges instead of walls, "I really value our relationship and want to make it even better, and I would like to discuss a concern that is important to me," is more likely to go over well than will the proverbial lead balloon: "You're going to have to change your character defects or else you're going to louse up our relationship."

5. *Help the Other.* Your associate's negative, demanding ways indicate that he or she is emotionally hurting. If he or she were hurting in a physical way, you would probably feel compassion. Although this is a different type of hurt, attempt to demonstrate an active sense of empathy for him or her. Sincere statements such as "You seem upset" or "It sounds like you were really given a hard time today; is there anything I can do to help?" may go a long way toward helping the person overcome overemotionalism. Compassionate understanding is a rare commodity; it tends to influence the person who is on the receiving end to gravitate more toward you and your values.

6. *Don't Rescue.* Try not to be an amateur social worker. Rescuing is when you try to do something for others that only they can do for themselves - for example, talking her out of how she feels, getting him to "see the light," or getting them to accept values and ideas that are obviously in their best interests. This is an impossible task that only will result in a lot of frustration because it won't be what the other person wants to hear. Instead, take a step backward rather than two steps forward and stubbornly refuse to believe that (a) you are responsible for others' problems and disturbances, and (b) that every problem has a perfect solution, which you must find for this individual.

7. *Become More Self-Interested.* Whether it be a marital partner, parent, child, employer, in-law, lover, or friend, unhappiness in that particular relationship doesn't mean that you and your entire life have to be miserable. Force yourself, if necessary, to pursue pleasurable activities for their own sake, apart from the troublesome relationship. Many times this will get the other's attention in a more positive way. By making yourself more happy in spite of it all, you will be more fun to be around and you may become more influential.

8. *Demonstrate That It Is in His or Her Best Interest to Change.* One of the best ways to teach anything is to model it. The ideas of "do as I say, not as I do" and "what is good for the goose isn't good for the gander" will not take hold in a relationship. By "biting the bullet" and refusing to allow yourself to be disturbed by the other's disturbance, you are modeling the advantages of emotional self-control. Over time, this patient, stoic effort can have an impact by demonstrating a less reactive, more fulfilling lifestyle.

It has been said that there are no guarantees in life other than death and taxes. However, by consistently using the steps outlined, you can increase, sometimes greatly, the probabilities of getting more of what you want and less of what you don't want in any given relationship. After you give it your best effort, you may find that at a minimum you have gained more disciplined, self-controlled philosophies and behaviors. At a maximum, you may also hit the relationship jackpot, producing the constructive type of influence you originally hoped for.

Note. From *Think Straight! Feel Great! 21 Guides to Emotional Self-Control* by Bill Borcherdt, ACSW, Copyright 1989, Professional Resource Exchange, Inc., P.O. Box 15560, Sarasota, FL 34277-1560.

You, Me, and Us:
Self-Interest Versus Selfishness

"Nothing is so powerful as an idea whose time has come" is an apt phrase for those who have not yet fully learned that it is blessed to give *and* receive, that self and social interests are not incompatible, and that putting oneself first and others a close second (rather than others first and self a distant second) can be better for all concerned. The value of self-interest is often misunderstood, not only to oneself but to those in one's social and family group. Selfishness is often mistakenly viewed as the Siamese twin of self-interest. This mistaken identity frequently leads to feelings of guilt, shame, and self-blame when acting on one's own behalf in one's own best interest. The goal of this guide is to make a flexible, well-thought-out distinction between these two close-sounding but opposite definitional ideas. The result of this review hopefully will be a more emotionally liberating, self-accepting, mentally healthy understanding of what one can realistically and responsibly expect of oneself in relationship to others.

Selfish behavior is seen as a purposeful effort to take something away from someone else, to deprive them of something that is legally and rightfully theirs, to benefit oneself at the expense of others, and to one-sidedly take with no expectation of giving in return. Such actions are both immoral and self-defeating because they work to the disadvantage of oneself and others. Selfish behaviors may achieve short-run goals, but in the long-run they usually backfire, alienating those with whom a selfish acting person associates.

Self-interest, in contrast, is a more enlightened concept. It keenly takes into consideration short- and long-term effects on all concerned. It points out the consequences of determinedly, unapologetically, and unashamedly striving for what you very strongly want without intending or doing harm to anyone else. After all, if you do what it takes to please yourself by actively and energetically seeking your vital interests, you are far more likely to: (a) be a happier individual; (b) be more fun to be around; (c) be kind, caring, and affectionate to those you love or would like to love; (d) be more in control of your own unique goals and values, while effectively aiding those who are less emotionally fortunate; and (e) be too busy and meaningfully absorbed in your vital, passionate undertakings to feel any significant degree of anger, anxiety, or other form of emotional disturbance. Your clearheadedness can serve as a model to those you may want to influence who may be less worry-free and unresentful than you.

Self-sacrificing individuals, who overconcern themselves with stepping on someone's toes, often mistake self-interested, self-directed activity for selfishness. This type of painstaking, guilt-ridden thinking frequently results in a desperate effort to please others and not appear too self-benefiting. Such an awkward display of self-giving heroics can also breed helplessness, dependency, and mutual resentment. Doing things for other people that they are capable of doing for themselves not only leads to mutual annoyance and even hatred, but these same self-deprivational, overly giving efforts are actually immoral. It is as immoral to hurt yourself with excessive altruism and self-sacrifice as it is to attempt to hurt others by intentionally slighting and depriving them. Consider the long-term effects of the parents who, instead of sensibly sharing their life with their child, end up sacrificing their life for their child; or the marital partner who gives until it hurts and then gives some more without believing in the right to expect anything in return; or the friend who permits others to take him or her for granted because of his or her seemingly endless giving ways. George Bernard Shaw spoke of the common denominator of such self-sacrificial relationships when he said, "If you start by sacrificing your life for those you love, you will end up hating those for whom you have sacrificed yourself."

Personal happiness and caring about others are not mutually exclusive goals. It is better to create your own enjoyment through pursuit of your own goals than to see your life as being for the pleasure of others, to direct as they see fit. Taking this more enlightened, broader perspective enables you to have a much more positive influence, not only on your own state of mind but on others with whom you associate. A self-interested philosophy is anything but selfish; its benefits extend beyond and filter through you to the others in your life.

Note. From *Think Straight! Feel Great! 21 Guides to Emotional Self-Control* by Bill Borcherdt, ACSW, Copyright 1989, Professional Resource Exchange, Inc., P.O. Box 15560, Sarasota, FL 34277-1560.

Guilt-Free Parenting

Parents are often led to believe that they determine the result of their child's adjustment. Much of the child development literature and many discussions about it suggest that parents are responsible if their child does not live up to community expectations or if his or her life does not turn out in an approved way. This type of thinking implies that parents of such children are to be blamed and condemned as being rotten, wicked, and villainous. In short, because of their child's "bad behavior," sometimes it is subtly or even openly insinuated that they are bad people who are less worthwhile as human beings.

This lopsided view of parent-child interaction is not only false but also encourages parents to wrongly believe they are on trial and that they must explain themselves, justify their decisions, and prove their good intentions to their self-styled critics (who sometimes are their own children). The net result is a lot of guilt-ridden parents who rate themselves according to their child's adjustment - who give themselves report cards with bad marks as people when their children have the *inevitable* problems children will have. As a consequence of their self-downing, parents don't problem-solve very effectively, are less in charge, find themselves "running scared," and sometimes perpetuate problems rather than create solutions. This guide attempts to help parents approach their responsibilities as enforcer, guide, and caregiver in a more unconditionally self-accepting, confident manner.

The following parent-advocacy model is designed to counter these defeating beliefs while increasing the strength and effectiveness of the parental role. This can be done by studying and reviewing each of the four following areas:

1. *Four Factors Beyond Parental Control:*

- *Genetic tendencies* toward disturbance and upsets. Not only do parents affect their kids, but kids in turn affect their parents. Children are born with temperamental differences and, although some children are harder to live with than others, by their nature they are all imperfect and fallible.
- *Peer group influences.* No matter how much tender love and care you give your children, they will look to their friends for even more acceptance and liking. Although some children seem to be more susceptible and vulnerable to peer persuasion than others and may require closer supervision, there are still parental limitations.
- *Influence of television and other media.* All humans are born with inclinations towards suggestibility, gullibility, and imitativeness. As P. T. Barnum once said, "There's a sucker born every minute." Truth in advertising is a myth and young people often unthinkingly accept hard- and soft-sell messages, however untrue they may be.
- *Societal changes.* Children have more rights than ever before. This can become a problem when the control factor is lacking. In jest, commentator Harry Reasoner once asked, "Should children who kill their parents get

orphan-survivor benefits?" Emphasis upon children's rights sometimes makes it difficult to assure that immediate, appropriate controls and discipline be administered following unacceptable behavior. Such lack of enforcement makes it difficult for children to learn from the consequences of their behavior, and makes the already difficult parent's job of enforcer even tougher.

2. *Children Interpret Things Differently.* Because of their own demandingness, biases, and prejudices - regardless of how good your intentions and how correct your methods - your children will see things the way they please. If you tell two different kids that they can't sleep over at a friend's house, one might view such limit-setting as meaning that you care enough to say "no." However, the second child may interpret your withholding a privilege as lack of love. The point is that, as a parent, you have no control over how your children think. It is best to take such fabricated thinking with a grain of salt lest you unknowingly give your children license to control your emotional well-being. Because of their basic controlling nature, most children would relish such an opportunity.

3. *Behavioral Tools to Resolve Parent-Child Conflicts in the Best Interests of Both.* These include listening skills, "I" position statements, workable compromises, and constructive use of consequences. Special attention is given to the importance of not mountain climbing over molehills while taking your child's criticisms less seriously. Also, parents need not think that they have to follow a recipe in the management and discipline of their child; instead they best be free to use their own judgment more spontaneously. This will more easily follow from a guilt-free, self-accepting, "I'm not on trial" attitude, as described in the next paragraph.

25

4. *Unconditional Self-Acceptance Training (USA).*
What USA means is that win, lose, or draw - in
parenting or in any other activity - you're still
the same person. You're not superhuman if
you succeed, nor subhuman if you don't accomplish your goals. Accepting yourself in spite
of your mistakes will usually result in making
fewer errors in the future, and regardless of
outcome, your value to yourself as a human being does not depend on your child's personal
and social adjustment.

Unconditional self-acceptance can be accomplished by analyzing, challenging, and uprooting mistaken ideas and philosophies about
parenting. Some of these irrational ideas include:

- "I should feel guilty when I say 'no' to my
  child or make errors in judgment that affect
  him."
- "My child must have at least one and preferably more outstanding abilities/special skills
  or talents for him to be personally satisfied,
  and for me to be satisfied with myself as a
  parent."
- "There has to be a perfect solution to my
  child's problems, and it is catastrophic if this
  perfect solution is not found."
- "It is necessary for my children to understand
  the reason, logic, and rationality behind the
  parenting decisions that I make, or they
  might think I don't love them and that would
  be horrible."
- "I must be thoroughly competent, adequate,
  and achieving as a parent to believe in my
  value to myself."
- "As a parent, I am responsible for whether
  my child conforms to community expectations, and deserve to be condemned by myself
  and others when this does not happen."
- "When my children feel unhappy it is my
  duty to show them the pathway to happiness,

and I must make myself disturbed when I don't succeed."

- "My children should appreciate me more than they actually do."
- "If my child wants to go to a foster home or run away, or if he or she compares me negatively to his or her friends' parents, it means I'm not giving enough love."
- "My children's early experiences determine their future because bad experiences will indefinitely influence their lives."
- "It would be awful if my child chose not to accept the values that I taught and believe in."
- "Children are born basically good, and therefore if they develop faults/negative traits early in life it must be my fault."
- "A parent's job responsibilities go on indefinitely."

Questioning and debating with yourself the validity of these false assumptions can go a long way toward emotional self-control and putting yourself "back into the driver's seat" as a parent. You might ask yourself the following questions:

- "Why do I have to feel guilty for being human enough to make mistakes?"
- "Why can't I instead try to make fewer mistakes in the future without condemning myself in the present?"
- "Why does every problem have to have a perfect solution, and why must I become unduly upset when exact answers are nowhere to be found?"
- "Why do I need my child's approval, and why is it so awful when he doesn't love me or threatens not to love me?"
- "Why must I do *the* best - why can't I do *my* best, and if that isn't good enough in the eyes of other people, why can't I just get on with life?"

- "Instead of feeling sorry for myself, why can't I simply accept the fact that my children often won't appreciate my efforts?"
- "What says that because things aren't right between my child and me, my whole life has to go down the tubes?"
- "Why can't I find pleasure and satisfaction in other areas of my life without bemoaning the problems my child has?"

Diagramming and using the ABCs of emotional re-education as invented by Albert Ellis (the founder of Rational-Emotive Therapy) can help parents master the means to more deliberately face the inevitable conflicts and frustrations of child-raising (see Table 1, pp. 30-31). For instance, at point A (activating event) your child goofs in some way - for example, fails in school, shoplifts, gets picked up for smoking pot, or all three! Frequently at point C (emotional consequences), the parent will feel guilty about the child's unacceptable behavior and wrongly believe that A caused C - for example, "My child's undesirable actions make me feel guilty and like a second-class citizen."

However, between A and C is B (beliefs about, interpretation of, A), and it is these self-statements that create the unwanted guilt feelings. These include such notions as: (a) "I should have done something to prevent this from happening, and therefore it is my fault." (b) "These problems are awful, terrible, and horrible, worse than anything else that could have happened." (c) "I can't stand myself nor these horrendous embarrassing circumstances, so I must get even more upset by what I can't stand - and if I can't stand something I have to be devastated by it." (d) "I stink! What a louse I am for letting such a lousy thing happen. I deserve to be blamed and condemned by self and others for being such a global no-good-nick!"

Such creation of a case for emotional upsettedness and self-downing leaves you ineffective not only in attempts to pick up the pieces as a parent, but also in other areas of your life. Self-control and self-acceptance in spite of your child's problem behaviors can best be achieved by instead moving to D (debate, dispute, self-argumentation) which challenges the B's listed above by self-stating provable, verifiable, hypotheses like these:

- "I can't follow my child around 24 hours a day." "I truly wish my son (or daughter) would have made wiser decisions about this matter, but it is impossible for me to make up his/her mind for him/her. There are limits to how much a parent can do, and like it or not, I had best accept this fact of life."
- "This situation is disappointing, but I don't have to turn it into a disaster by making it bigger than life."
- "This is nothing that I have to be ashamed of."
- "This is a sorrowful circumstance, and I may even have done some asinine things to contribute to it. I am a fallible, imperfect human, and I will accept myself regardless of my flubs, though I will try like hell to flub less in the future. To think otherwise will only result in upsetting myself about something that has already happened and can't be changed."

The benefits of relentlessly, forcefully, and ruthlessly making such statements will be an updated, more sensible, and more tolerant philosophy/belief system which will allow you as a parent to think more clearly and accept yourself more humanly. You will then be more likely to use your parent-effectiveness tools in a way that better serves both you and your child.

The view described in this guide is designed to bring a sense of humility to the parental role. It humanistically puts parents more at the center of their universe by allowing them to not let their child's problems dictate feelings of guilt, shame, anger, embarrassment, or depression. Being able to forgive yourself for being an imperfect parent

TABLE 1: REVIEW OF THE ABCs OF PARENT EMOTIONAL RE-EDUCATION

Activating Event	Beliefs, Interpretations, Self-Talk about A	Emotional Consequences	Forcefully Self-Argue, Dispute, Debate the B's	New Effects
A	B	C	D	E
Child gets into trouble - for example, fails in school, shop-lifts, gets picked up for smoking pot.	"I should have done some-thing to prevent this from happening."	Guilt	"Who says I have to, why must I, how can I follow my son/daughter around 24 hours a day! flexibly."	Feel better, think more clearly and
	"These problems are awful, terrible, and shamefully bad."		"Why do I have to turn a disappointing circum-stance into a disaster?"	Problem-solve more effectively or better able to gracefully accept not find-ing a solution.

Activating Event	Beliefs, Interpretations, Self-Talk about A	Emotional Consequences	Forcefully Self-Argue, Dispute, Debate the B's	New Effects
A	B	C	D	E
	"I can't stand this situation, I can't stand myself for letting my child get in such a mess."		"I don't have to be ashamed about anything under the sun!"	
	"I stink! What a louse I am for letting such a lousy thing happen - I deserve to be blamed and condemned as a global no-good-nick."		"I am a fallible, imperfect human being, and I will give myself 'undamning acceptance' regardless of my flubs, though I will try like hell to make fewer flubs in the future."	

of an imperfect child is one of the most lofty and productive goals to be sought during these brief, guiding, enforcing, and caregiving years.

Note. From *Think Straight! Feel Great! 21 Guides to Emotional Self-Control* by Bill Borcherdt, ACSW, Copyright 1989, Professional Resource Exchange, Inc., P.O. Box 15560, Sarasota, FL 34277-1560.

Failure Redefined: Is It Really Bigger Than Life and the Worst of All Possible Crimes?

A client of mine, after attempting a homework assignment between sessions, stated somewhat tongue-in-cheek: "Bill, I tried everything you told me to do and none of it worked - but I feel better." Her paradoxical statement brought to mind the reality that failure, like success, is not all it's cracked up to be. One of the problems with success is that little is learned from it. On the other hand, as Ben Franklin once said, "That which hurts, instructs," whereas Nietzsche put it another way: "That which does not kill me makes me stronger."

Failure means many things that don't meet the eye:

1. Be glad you're failing, because it shows you're trying - involved in life rather than withdrawing from it.
2. By trying, you're sending yourself the message that you think you have value to yourself. Such efforts are in themselves strengthening and motivating. If you succeed with this added persistence, it will be frosting on the cake, because the perseverance against odds has value in and of itself.

3. Failure is frequently the short-term price you pay for long-term success. Much learning comes from trial-and-error efforts; going down blind alleys is a frequent prerequisite for finding one's way home. An advantage to such experiential, reality-based understanding is that lessons tend to be remembered longer following such adversity. It often takes 10 or 20 years to become an "overnight" success, and the wisdom that stems from really pushing yourself toward direct exposure to potential failures can provide life-long benefits of self-understanding, self-actualization, as well as concrete learning.

4. Dogged determination to take on a spirited, adventuresome, risk-taking outlook leads to vital absorption in life. Following your unique bents, inklings, and leanings, and challenging yourself to become emotionally immersed in a special interest, task, or activity without assurance of success, can give special meaning to life. A successful result can have special value, but it is the affirmation of your values from your own creative efforts that is truly rewarding.

5. Failure cannot be avoided by not trying. On the contrary, failure is more assured by not trying. A coward dies many times; a person who believes in himself or herself and acts upon those beliefs dies only once. One cannot *not* make a decision; to decide not to try is to maintain the status quo.

6. Although life is not fair and does not consistently provide what one deserves, one can succeed by failing in doing the immediate right thing but still get desirable long-term results. It doesn't necessarily follow that good things only happen to people who succeed or that bad things only happen to those who fail. One can take a wrong turn only to find out later that a traffic jam was avoided by doing so, say the wrong thing and still get the promotion,

fumble the ball on the opponent's 5-yard line only to have a teammate recover it in the end zone for a touchdown, or flounder in other human ways only to open up new contacts, opportunities, and avenues for future reference.

7. Failing encourages you to remember your humble beginnings - to become a more compassionate, tolerant, accepting, forgiving human being, with a finer appreciation for those less fortunate. Being directly exposed to your own fallibilities and imperfections discourages the human tendency toward self-righteousness and general psychological one-upmanship.

8. Nonsuccessful experiences provide a golden opportunity to work against natural low-frustration tolerance tendencies. Because of limited time, resources, and opportunities, many of life's sought-after benefits and goals will remain out of reach for most people. Striving for what you want, though unfortunately failing to achieve your objectives, extends your capacities to accept this grim reality. Because happiness is a direct ratio between what you expect and what you get, and because failure encourages and trains you to expect less, more long-range happiness is better insured by failure experiences.

9. Failure exposes you to the option of accepting yourself regardless - win, lose, or draw. Long-run ego anxiety and self-blaming tendencies can be minimized by not insisting on proving yourself.

10. Adversity stemming from failure can be good for overall personal development. Looking back on the saddest, most regretful time of your life will typically yield meaningful revelations that enhance your life's quality and intensity. "Never depriving a child of the right to go without" will encourage the push to expand boundaries, to discover and more fully utilize inherent potential. The best personal capaci-

ties often emerge from the worst life circumstances.

If failure both reveals and builds stronger-willed, more self-actualized human beings, why is it often viewed as so frightening? Why do most people go to such extremes to avoid, rationalize, and deny its presence, while insisting upon, demanding, and lusting after success? The sanctification of success and condemnation of failure can be traced to two separate yet related phenomena:

1. *Irrational Beliefs As Manufactured by Individuals.* Irrational beliefs are thoughts that cannot be supported by evidence. Such unverifiable thinking leads to unwanted, choice-blocking emotions that cause inaction or underactivity on the one hand, or counterproductive over-reaction on the other hand. There are four main categories of unsubstantiated notions that cause emotional paralysis and behavioral avoidance:

   - The fear of failure as awful, devastating, impossible to cope with, and therefore without any possible benefits.
   - The insistence on success or exceptional performance: such demanding, all-or-nothing thinking results in becoming emotionally bound up because of unrealistic expectations and, ironically, less able to attain desirable goals and cope with one's inevitable fallibility and imperfection.
   - Self-statements implying that some humans are more worthwhile than others: such unprovable assumptions encourage self-rating games when one believes that practical advantages for succeeding confer status as a better person. Desperately depending on the fruits of your labors for self-acceptance feeds fragile self-confidence and encourages over-concern, self-consciousness, and distraction from the task at hand.

- Need statements that result in the belief that success is essential: such arbitrary requirements for happiness and survival create a lot of internal pressure and obstruct the clear-headed thinking required to reach desired objectives.

2. *Intertwined with Irrational Thinking Is the Human Tendency to Overgeneralize from a Limited Data Sampling.* This inclination contributes to many ideas about failure avoidance, including these:

- "If I fail in what I do, I fail in who I am."
- "If something, like success, is good, I *have to* experience it."
- "If something, like failure, is bad, I *must* avoid experiencing it."
- "If something, like failure, has frequently occurred, it *has to* continue to occur." This idea contributes to a hopeless, demotivating philosophy.
- "Something that is sad, regretful, disappointing, depriving, or inconveniencing is intolerable and therefore disastrous."

These two interrelated categories of irrational and overgeneralized leanings are invented self-statements that inflict a petrification of failure and thereby increase the possibility. As William Shakespeare once said, "Nothing is so horrible but that thinking makes it so." Redefining failure by unshackling dogmatic, rigid rules of living while easing preconceived ideas about the human inevitability of floundering would be a very good start towards a happier, more freeing philosophy. The next step is forced, prompted action aimed at actually *doing repeatedly* what you have fearfully avoided. Such massed, sustained practice will likely smoke out nutty, self-defeating ideas that have blocked self-choosing initiative and have made failure seem demoralizing, unyielding, and all-important.

It may seem more immediately convenient to avoid all appearances of failure by going with the current rather than fighting upstream against it. However, taking this short-range view of life prevents one from gaining possible long-range success, or at least touching base with the satisfaction of attempting a job well done. By utilizing one of the disputational techniques of Rational-Emotive Therapy - rational debate with oneself - one can restate self-sabotaging, self-terrorizing thinking. Contrasting one's thinking will allow for different, more invigorating emotions, in turn inviting productive action. There are four dimensions to this self-challenging, self-argumentative tool:

1. Write on one side of a piece of paper all the irrational beliefs (IBs) you cling to when frightening yourself about possible failure. Draw an arrow from each IB to the other side of the paper, where you write self-disputational, rational countering belief (RCBs). To illustrate:

IBs

- "I have to succeed."
- "I must not fail."
- "Trying and failing would be catastrophic, terrible, awful, horrible."
- "Failure is intolerable, unbearable - I can't stand it."
- "If I try I might fail, and if I failed I'd be a louse, so I'll avoid failure and lousehood by not trying."

RCBs

- "It's true I'd like to, want to, would prefer to succeed and would probably find success quite delightful, but where is the evidence that I have to do what I find desirable?"

- "Is it really a cosmic truth that I cannot, must not fail? In fact, is there really any proof that anything in life has to be? Success may bring me advantages but what does it really get me to insist upon gaining these same advantages?"
- "It may be correct that trying and failing would be disappointing, but would such a deficiency really be bigger than life and result in the world no longer spinning on its axis?"
- "My survival does not depend upon succeeding, and though I may be inconvenienced, frustrated, and deprived by failing, can't I learn from my shortcoming and go on with my life?"
- "If I try I might fail, but does my failure really turn me into a blameworthy human being whose self-value is diminished? Or am I merely overstating the significance of failure, and jumping to conclusions about myself in relationship to my floundering?"

2. Now, actively, vigorously, and in no-nonsense terms carry forth a personal debate where you first present each irrational argument, and in turn dispute every single misconception listed. To get more meaningful results, do this self-argumentative project out loud. How you talk to others affects them; how you talk to yourself affects you. To give yourself feedback on how self-convincing you are, tape the self-dialogue and then listen to the intensity of your delivery. Because spontaneity comes from mastery of skills, the more frequently and intently you practice this self de-indoctrination exercise, the more natural the sensible ideas will be.
3. Practice with a confederate who will play the role of a devil's advocate, stating one at a time your listed irrational notions. You then will try to talk your companion out of "your" ir-

rational beliefs as he or she presents them. This spirited practice arrangement will give you the opportunity to talk someone else out of your crooked thinking, encouraging the value of thinking for yourself in a way that will allow you to feel more the way you want to feel and less the way you don't want to feel.

4. Give yourself behavioral assignments permitting you to act against your (up until now) self-sabotaging thoughts that lead to fear and inaction. The best way to change your irrational beliefs about failure is to act against them. It is easy to stay afraid of something you avoid; it's difficult to remain frightened of what has been faced.

The perspectives gained beyond possible success and positively confronted failure have intrinsic value and make life more intensely meaningful. Valuing, savoring, and focusing on the *process* of your efforts will free you up to pursue the products you treasure from life in a less anxious and more joyful and motivated manner.

Note. From *Think Straight! Feel Great! 21 Guides to Emotional Self-Control* by Bill Borcherdt, ACSW, Copyright 1989, Professional Resource Exchange, Inc., P.O. Box 15560, Sarasota, FL 34277-1560.

Resisting Practically Anything, Including Temptation: Overcoming Low Frustration Tolerance

"A person is rich in direct proportion to the number of things that he can afford to go without." Given the truth of this seeming paradoxical statement, why is it that depriving oneself and being deprived, frustrated, and/or inconvenienced is so difficult to accept? This guide focuses on why low frustration tolerance (LFT) and deprivation anxiety are such common occurrences, how they are created as emotional problems, and more importantly, what can be done about them.

George Bernard Shaw identified two tragedies in life, "not getting your heart's desire, and getting your heart's desire." Even if you are born with a silver spoon in your mouth, you are likely to encounter frustrations, obstacles, and barriers to personal happiness and self-fulfillment.

Low frustration tolerance (LFT) may not be as dramatic as other emotional problems such as anger, fear, guilt, or depression, but often more pervasively and consistently blocks one's happiness and sabotages one's goals. In fact, it may be the most obvious and comprehensive, yet most frequently overlooked malady that humans have. It frequently causes emotional problems and practically always seems to infiltrate and escalate existing disturbances and upsets. Identifying and understanding this self-actualization-blocking enemy is important to happiness.

Frustration starts with a perceptual gap or error - a discrepancy between what you expected and what you actually got. Dieting didn't turn out to be as easy as you thought it would be; your associate didn't treat you with the kindness and consideration you expected; your own performance turned out to be at a lower level than you originally anticipated; or you did not gain as complete a control of your feelings as you would have liked. This is emotionally healthy and normal because without any degree of frustration, it is unlikely that you would be motivated to actively strive for your goals. The only way to completely avoid frustration is to not value anything, which would probably result in boredom and eventual depression.

LFT is the amplification of this original frustration leading to a multiplying effect. Reacting to one's original frustration creates emotional havoc and self-defeating behavior. Definitive descriptions of this encompassing, prevalent phenomenon are:

1. Exaggerating the emotional pain that you are required to go through to achieve a given result.
2. Making yourself feel undisciplined, lethargic, listless, hopeless, and helpless by whining and screaming because life is not always convenient and things are just too hard to put up with.
3. Babying yourself by taking a short-range view of life, overfocusing on the immediate discomfort of a given effort to the neglect of longer-range benefits.
4. Pouting, self-pitying, moaning, and groaning about the varied inequities and injustices in life.
5. Agonizing about your incapacity to attain your desired goals or achieve at preferred levels.

42

6. Theatrically complaining about being treated poorly or unfairly.
7. Arguing bitterly with yourself about your own feelings and the absolute horror of not being able to control them.
8. Bleakly and histrionically describing your disenchantment with things in your natural environment that inconvenience you, such as the weather, bumpy roads, traffic congestion, or high taxes.
9. Dwelling on the asinine way others act, including but not limited to elected government officials, colleagues, friends, family, mate, or lovers.
10. Catastrophizing about how terrifying and wretched it is that matters of preference in life are not precise and predictable.
11. Under-reactiveness is an often overlooked version of LFT involving a nonchalant attitude that underestimates the difficulty of the task at hand. Purposeful minimizing essential effort can really cover-up feelings of high frustration and provide a disguised rationalization for inaction. After all, if something is such a snap to accomplish, it's hardly worth putting forth the effort. Hidden beneath this apparent low-key, laid-back philosophy is a view that the world is too tough, and any energy directed toward goal attainment is seen as asking too much and not worth the effort.

Having a low threshold for emotional pain is not often viewed as an appealing topic for furthering self-understanding, perhaps because of the "doing what comes easiest" philosophy that frequents our culture. Yet, if the brakes aren't slammed on "comfort-junkie" inclinations, a pyramiding effect will quickly escalate life's hassles into seeming horrors. Taking the original frustration and running with it can be seen in the following self-statements:

- "It's awful."
- "I can't stand it."
- "I couldn't tolerate that."
- "Nothing is worse than that."
- "What a disaster."
- "That's horrifying."
- "How terrifying."
- "I was mortified."
- "That would ruin and destroy me."
- "It's way too hard."

Any or all of these low frustration tolerance philosophies will likely result in either (a) impulsively doing the wrong thing because you "can't stand" certain things and end up breaking a diet, going off an exercise program, telling somebody off, exiting a job or relationship prematurely, or spending money you don't have; or (b) putting off doing the right thing because "it's too hard," such as starting a diet or an exercise program, making a decision, telling someone how you feel, applying for a job, seeking a promotion, or going after that unique relationship you would like to have. Such self-defeating actions or inactions tie into several overgeneralized beliefs that may start with a valid, factual premise but end with an illogical, fictional conclusion:

- "I'm not getting my own way, and that's awful and overburdening."
- "Life isn't fair, and thus I can't stand it."
- "Something is good and desirable so I have to have it, and it's terrible if I don't get it."
- "Something is bad and undesirable so it must not happen to me, and it would be unbearable if it did."

Or, they may begin with a false premise and lead into what appears to be a logical conclusion:

- "Something is unbearable; therefore I can hardly expect to cope effectively."

- "I have to have my own way, so there is a good possibility that I will get extremely frustrated, if not downright sulky, during times I don't."
- "Certain things should not happen to me, and I can't stand it when they do, so I'm certainly going to be overwhelmed if they occur."
- "I need and must have certain advantages in life and should not have certain other disadvantages; I am likely to decompensate if I am forced to settle for the short end of the stick."

All these varying versions of self-aggravations that dramatize and exaggerate disappointments and inconveniences frequently affect task expectancies, as well as self-development and interpersonal efforts, thereby also escalating rather than remediating existing problems. Because LFT sabotages even the best of intentions, release from these common, self-imposed restraints would permit a higher quality of emotional life and greater personal satisfaction. The following suggestions might further this goal:

1. Voltaire once said, "One great use of words is to fight your own thoughts." Start by identifying your irrational ideas, and then forcefully argue and debate with yourself against these self-defeating notions. For instance, strongly ask yourself such self-confrontational disputations as: "Where is the evidence that something bad is intolerable?"; "Why can't I stand what I don't like?"; "Is this really such a disaster, or is it really just one of life's regrettable, undelightful, inevitable disappointments?" Because humans have LFT regarding unwanted thoughts, feelings, and/or behavior, self-arguments best deal with emotions such as anger, guilt, and depression, as well as pesty thoughts that you have been unable to shake.

2. Transpose your most powerful and effective self-instructional statements onto a note card that you can carry and review aloud to yourself several times daily.

3. Put these same self-arguments on tape and listen to yourself think out loud rationally.
4. Practice rational-emotive imagery by picturing yourself very vividly and clearly in a difficult life circumstance. Then force yourself to experience your typical LFT feelings such as listlessness, anxiety, fear, and inertia. Finally, force yourself to change those same choice-blocking feelings to more motivating, adrenalin-flowing, appropriately apprehensive feelings while envisioning the same problem circumstance. Riding these emotional blocks will better create the perspiration from which the inspiration can flow.
5. Openly and unashamedly reveal to others your LFT tendencies and your plans to actively work against them.
6. Use "Grandma's Rule" on yourself: contract with yourself to do something that's difficult yet beneficial, but about which you have LFT, before allowing yourself a more pleasurable activity. For example, do your dictation, monthly reports, or term paper before you watch television; exercise before you allow yourself to participate in your favorite hobby or read the newspaper.
7. Penalize yourself if you do not meet your self-imposed time deadline for completing the difficult, though desirable task. Penalties might include such obnoxious tasks as cleaning out the toilet three times, calling a person you dislike and patronizing him or her, or getting up an hour earlier the next day.
8. Really force yourself to act against the self-created nonsense that says that certain situations may yield terrible, intolerable results. As Bertrand Russell once suggested, familiarity will tend to blunt the terrors of that which is considered fearsome.

A client of mine once resignfully stated, "I'll have LFT on my tombstone." He was failing to see his choice in the matter. You can go to your grave kicking and screaming about life's difficulties and unfairness, or you can take on a more determined, tough-minded view that allows for the acceptance of life's annoying inconveniences. This level-headed perspective may be difficult to accomplish, but consistent under- or over-reaction to life's experiences is even harder. Deliberately responding rather than desperately reacting to circumstances will lead to greater riches than short-range comfort or temptation can provide.

Note. From *Think Straight! Feel Great! 21 Guides to Emotional Self-Control* by Bill Borcherdt, ACSW, Copyright 1989, Professional Resource Exchange, Inc., P.O. Box 15560, Sarasota, FL 34277-1560.

Self-Esteem As Disturbance

Increasing self-esteem is a goal that virtually all self-help movements vigorously pursue with good intentions. Yet, if words like self-esteem, self-concept, and self-worth are closely examined, what is found is that they lead to an escalation rather than remediation of emotional disturbance. The premise of this guide is that "self-esteem enhancement" with self and others has many overlooked and pernicious side effects.

Rating or esteeming oneself for special reasons runs counter to human happiness and emotional stability. "I'm a good person because . . ." leads to patting oneself on the back when doing the right thing, but also to "I'm a bad person because . . ." with a kicking oneself in the behind, when inevitably doing the wrong thing. It is as silly to measure oneself favorably when right as it is to negatively categorize oneself when wrong - humans *do* their behavior but they *are not* their behavior.

Granted, controlling for success and "the good things in life" may result in your being better off, and not controlling for what is desired may bring disadvantages, but you are the same person regardless of outcome.

Proclaiming "self-esteem" usually means, "I am a nut who has to like myself usually for things that I do well and for others' favorable comments about me." Somehow my positive characteristics, traits, features that I have and the affirmations and the validations I receive make me more worthwhile. This form of self-measurement eventually will lead to self-blame, self-downing, and emotional disturbance while antihumanistically making internal conditions more susceptible to external circumstances. It encourages its true believers to go after the right thing - for example, love, wellness, approval - for the wrong reason - because they think their affirmations and accomplishments make them better, more worthwhile people. As a consequence, the promoters of self-esteem feel better but get worse. Even if you get what you "have to have" to hold your self-esteem in place, you will tend to feel anxious about the possibility of losing these self-defined essential requirements. You become damned if you do, and damned if you don't accomplish whatever it takes to gain the treasured self-esteem. This rating system therefore often creates the very upsets it attempts to abolish.

What is the solution? Question your assumptions about what self-esteem and personal worth mean to you. Throw out definitions that imply that some humans are more worthwhile and more "esteemed" than others. Stop playing the rating game where you give yourself a report card with a good or bad mark. Then opt for a broader, more comprehensive concept called unconditional self-acceptance (USA).

Self-acceptance differs from self-esteem by allowing you to accept yourself without any external props or conditions. You can be yourself without having to prove yourself. You accept yourself with the problem first, and then, because it would be to your advantage, work persistently and relentlessly to solve it. It allows you to fully accept yourself without needing justification, and teaches that if you accept yourself in spite of your blunders, you will probably goof less. Unlike pursuing self-esteem, you are protected emotionally if others select against or don't validate you, or if you make a mistake. Self-esteem is a junk word that contributes to emotional indigestion. If you pass judgment on yourself, your emotional health is up for grabs.

Self-esteem is a concept that doesn't promote human growth and development. It is the quest for rather than the conquest of self-esteem that can cause rather than cure emotional disturbance. Self-esteem is the devil in disguise in that anytime you pass judgment on yourself, whether it be a good or bad, you lose emotional self-control. This type of ego, self-rating scale leads to a despisement rather than an acceptance of self.

It is a gross oversimplification of the complexity of human beings to say that "low self-esteem" is at the foundation of almost all emotional disturbance and self-defeating behavior. One more pervasive, though less dramatic factor may be low frustration tolerance (LFT) or the inability to restrain and deprive oneself or to accept frustration. It is true that *after* you overeat, err in hitting your child, or falter in judgment in some other way, you may down yourself for such an unesteemed act. But again, such self-flagellation or low self-esteem is a by-product and *not* the cause of the original mistake.

Fortunately, humans are human and are not rats or guinea pigs. They can recognize that happiness is not externally caused. They can think for themselves in ways that will permit a more self-accepting, clear-thinking view of themselves and their relationships with others. They can better control their own emotional destiny by fully acknowledging ever-present human fallibilities and imperfections in a truly nonjudgmental, "unesteemed," more fully humanistic way.

Note. From *Think Straight! Feel Great! 21 Guides to Emotional Self-Control* by Bill Borcherdt, ACSW, Copyright 1989, Professional Resource Exchange, Inc., P.O. Box 15560, Sarasota, FL 34277-1560.

To Be or Not to Be Angry

Of all the human emotions, anger has created the most harm and caused the greatest destruction within individuals, couples, families, and between social groups and nations. The vengefulness caused by anger usually results in "cutting off one's nose to spite one's face," as it is impossible to hate, despise, or resent somebody without suffering oneself. Anger has many two-edged advantages, such as: (a) providing a feeling of strength and power; (b) creating the illusion that you are doing something constructive about your problem when you are really making it worse; (c) supplying feelings of superiority; (d) substituting for feeling hurt and rejection; and (e) allowing you to think anything you want to about the other person without danger of retaliation. These aloof, all-mighty feelings build walls instead of bridges, result in lost opportunities, lead to physical abuse and legal complications, and can be a health hazard by contributing to ulcers or high blood pressure, to name a few drawbacks.

There are at least four major myths or mistaken ideas about anger: (a) it is externally caused; (b) the best way to deal with it is to express it openly, directly, and "constructively"; (c) it can be a helpful, useful, beneficial emotion; and (d) if you don't get angry you have to play the "patsy," become someone else's "psychological slave," or otherwise let yourself get taken advantage of or be abused. Let's examine these four assumptions.

MYTH NUMBER ONE

Somebody or something outside of you magically gets into your gut and makes you angry or gets you upset. Happiness or unhappiness is not externally caused; like all human emotions, anger is self-created. Anger usually occurs when someone else thinks, feels, or acts in ways you don't think he or she "should," and you want to teach him or her a lesson or retaliate. There are three main components of anger:

1. *Demandingness.* The notion that you run the universe and others should not violate your laws on how it should operate. Like it or not, others have a right to do the wrong thing, to think for themselves, and follow their own minds. Even after you have treated someone with kindness, courtesy, and consideration, he or she is not obligated to return the favor.

   Also, although you may dislike and disapprove of others' objectionable, irritating, and annoying traits, it's best not to think that because they "could" be different, therefore they "should." A should is a demand, and demandingness is at the center of human disturbance. It is your protest against the others' behavior and not the behavior itself that gives you your anger problems.

2. *Condemnation.* The mistaken view that people who do the wrong thing or don't do the right thing are to be condemned as rotten, wicked, villainous individuals. This other downing notion readies one to plan psychological or physical revenge.

3. *Punitive Action.* Because others are such awful, wicked people for committing such awful, wicked deeds, they deserve to be punished as a

54

reminder of their sins so they don't make the same mistakes again. However, if punishment were a deterrent to negative acts, there would be much less repeated crime. Punishment intends to harm the other person in some way, directly or indirectly, and it is these demanding, condemning, and punitive tendencies that actually create anger.

MYTH NUMBER TWO

Expressing your anger solves or gets rid of it. When you express your anger, you feel better for the moment but you don't *get* any better; in fact, in the long-run you may get worse. Asserting yourself angrily, hitting pillows, or screaming at the top of your lungs does more harm than good, because feelings of anger get practiced and reinforced by such behaviors. Such "spewing out" doesn't get at your core irrational beliefs: that others have to meet your requirements and don't have a right to be wrong.

MYTH NUMBER THREE

Anger can be a helpful, useful, beneficial emotion. Getting yourself angry may get you your own way more often, but once the dust has settled from your emotional explosion, you will probably pay a costly price in terms of relationship strain and disruption. If you act like a porcupine, others are likely to get the message and start to avoid you. Besides, when you get yourself angry at someone who treats you negatively, you repeat the other's mistake and act out the very behaviors you claim to despise. Two wrongs beget two wrongs, not a right.

MYTH NUMBER FOUR

If you don't get angry and counterattack, you become "the patsy," someone else's "psychological slave," or somehow a weak or inferior person. On the contrary, it takes someone who is secure and well-grounded not to automatically get upset in the face of someone else's wrath. Decide for yourself how you want to feel and not how someone else is going to "make you" feel. Don't allow yourself to get disturbed about someone else's disturbance. Express yourself if you choose, but in a more settled way. Firm, simple, self-directed statements such as "I disagree," "I don't like that," "I don't want that," "I don't want that to happen again," or "I want to think about that first" will allow you to make your position known in a more productive, less threatening manner.

If at point A (activating event) someone criticizes you or treats you unfairly, and at point C (emotional consequences) you begin to feel angry, don't assume that A is causing C. Examine what you are telling yourself at B (beliefs about A), because it is these self-sentences and preconceived ideas that you are upsetting yourself with. Chances are you are starting to tell yourself, "He shouldn't act that way," "He has no right," or "What a louse he is for acting lousily - now I must get even and teach him a lesson he will not soon forget."

As soon as you identify these internalized, unprovable statements, go on to D (debate, dispute). Strongly question and dispute these ideas with such truthful arguments as, "Why shouldn't he do the wrong thing?" "Why doesn't he have the right to be wrong?" "Why is it so awful, and why can't I stand unkind treatment?" "Why is he a bad person for acting badly? He is an imperfect human being who is obviously having a hard time living with himself right now, and I need not upset myself about his anger."

This type of strong, vigorous, rational self-talk will take you to E (new effects). You won't feel great because the other is treating you negatively, but you won't feel that the world is coming to an end because of his or her lapses in kindness, either. At E you will achieve more tolerant views, feel less upset in the face of irritating and annoying acts, and be better able to influence and change what was originally happening at A, if you wish.

To overcome anger, dispute your demanding definitions of how you insist others treat you. When you find yourself in disfavor with another, challenge those inventions and fictions about how others "should," "must," and "ought to" act toward you. Despite occasional, forgivable lapses, if you consistently and thoroughly own up to the facts about anger, you will find yourself with fewer axes to grind, getting angry less often, and more permanently believing that life is too short to have it any other way.

Note. From *Think Straight! Feel Great! 21 Guides to Emotional Self-Control* by Bill Borcherdt, ACSW, Copyright 1989, Professional Resource Exchange, Inc., P.O. Box 15560, Sarasota, FL 34277-1560.

Perfectionism and the
Pursuit of Unhappiness

Perfectionistic ambitions are a lot like trying to fight city hall and win. Such strivings are a full-time job, burn up excessive energy, and in the end are most frustrating and unlikely to succeed. Yet such unrealistic, exacting objectives seem to be the rule rather than the exception in human goal-setting. Perfectionistic acting people follow their insistent demands to the hilt and futilely attempt to be superhuman, only to run head-on into their fallible humanity, leaving them unhappy and creating aggravation for all. This guide defines this addictive pursuit, earmarks its aspects and impact on the human condition, addresses its causes, and suggests ways to minimize its negative effect on personal happiness. After all, it's most unlikely that you will ever be perfect at anything, including completely eliminating your perfectionism!

Simply stated, perfectionism demands that people or circumstances be different than they actually are. It mirrors inflexible, all-or-nothing thinking that paralyzes one's emotions, and to that extent it is frequently found at the center of emotional disturbance. In short, it is a protest against reality, a refusal to accept what exists.

Being human is synonymous with being fallible and imperfect, so why this pursuit against impossible odds? Possible reasons include the following:

1. There are genetic tendencies to lust for everlasting assurances, certainties, and predictability. This innate disposition runs counter to a world that issues virtually no guarantees and leads to perhaps the ultimate self-defeating activity. Some humans have stronger tendencies toward perfectionism than others, and natural perfectionistic strivings quickly escalate socially taught and approved preferences into demands: "Because it's good and beneficial, I have to be perfectly achieving in having a well-paying job, a satisfying love and sex life, and so on."

   Like all inclinations, perfectionism presents a strong leaning but is not binding. With hard work it can be acted against, and its undesirable effects on everyday living can be minimized.

2. Perfectionistic strivings are an attempt, however futile, to cover up mounting feelings of anxiety when people, things, or events don't meet defined expectations. Being perfect becomes a safety factor - a prerequisite for feeling comfortable. Paradoxically, the quest for everyone and everything being in its proper place multiplies the anxious feelings that accompany insisting upon the impossible: the prescription becomes the illness, and the cure becomes worse than the disease.

3. Secondary perfectionistic problems occur when such efforts fail to camouflage feelings of inferiority, as originally intended. Perfectionistic acting people frequently feel inferior to begin with, and try to conceal and compensate for such self-diminishing notions by proving themselves to be beyond reproach - they are not satisfied to simply be themselves. At its core, perfectionism is an ego problem that begins with a self-blaming tendency and ends with

even more self-downing when one cannot exactly control for a given result. Falling short of the mark is equated with worthlessness.

Perfectionism has many dimensions, mirrored in its following components:

1. *Personal Performance.* The idea that I have to do the best in whatever activity, project, or goal I attempt. Included here is a belief in the success ethic that says, "I have to do better than everybody else and better than the last time I did it, or else I'm no damned good." This philosophy of perfectionistic self-blame frequently contains a double standard: "It's all right for my associates to make mistakes - after all, to err is human - but because I have to prove what an ultra-grand individual I am, I'm not allowed that luxury." This conceited, sometimes subtle ideal is often hidden behind the more obvious self-blaming.

2. *Others' Performance.* Trying to control others builds walls rather than bridges. Yet this is just what a perfectionistic, other-controlling acting person attempts to do. Instead of flexibly accepting the realities of human variability and individual differences, the perfectionistically demanding person rigidly maintains that "everyone is entitled to my opinion," and that free will really means "my will."

3. *Life's Circumstances.* The insistence that life's conditions be fair, deserving, providing, and convenient runs counter to the actual objectivity and impartiality by which the universe seems to operate. The perfectionist tries to personally control for orderly, preferential treatment.

4. *Ultra Control of One's Own Feelings.* Refusal to accept that humans are not chronically happy, are not robots, and are not equipped to turn feelings off and on creates a problem about the problem. The perfectionistic overfocus on

feeling differently than one actually does at a given point in time will cause unwanted feelings to intensify and linger rather than naturally run their course. In becoming more emotionally bound up, discomfort about the discomfort begins to increase. This mushrooming effect will continue until you accept your natural fallibility in controlling your own feelings, or until emotional exhaustion sets in.

5. *Controlling for Others' Happiness.* Altruistic, self-sacrificing notions that every problem of significant others has a perfect solution that you are totally responsible for finding takes its own emotional toll. Attempting to do others' work for them in meeting their wishes and wants will often result in getting caught up in someone else's spiral of emotional disturbance.

6. *Unacceptable Thoughts and Images.* Frozen definitions about the thoughts and images that you "should," "must," or "ought to" have frequently cause feelings of guilt and self-diminishment. Worrying, vengefulness, or pity may be a waste of time, but dwelling and obsessing about having these thinking patterns is even worse than experiencing them.

7. *Perplexing Physical Sensations or Other Sudden, Momentary, Unpleasant States.* Reacting to one's reactions such as heart palpitations, momentary dizziness, brief unexplainable aches and pains, irritating hot flashes, queasy sensations, flashbacks, dreams, or nightmares with the perfectionistic self-command, "I must not feel this way - how awful" can again cause original problems to be extended rather than contained.

8. *Decision Making.* Trying to find out tomorrow's answers today profoundly stifles one's energy. Believing that one must make the perfect decision that will be universally fair can cause one to end up like the donkey who was an equal distance from two hay stacks, but ended up starving to death because he couldn't decide from which to eat. As one of my cli-

ents said about a choice I asked him to make, "I'll give you a definite maybe."

9. *Body Image.* What is typically portrayed as a health concern can become an obsession with maintaining a perfect body image to impress others. In short, "my deficiencies at maintaining a perfect physique are the same as my worthlessness as a human being." As in other perfectionistic pursuits, the attempt at psychological one-upmanship leads to psychological self-downing.

10. *Approval Seeking.* Thinking that "others' opinions equal me" and that value to oneself cannot be gained apart from others' affirmation results in trying to be all things to all people rather than accepting oneself. The need to be the perfect people-pleaser inevitably paves the way for a letdown when no specific way of being suits everybody.

11. *Achieving Perfect Rationality.* Many who are currently in or have had therapy, and other psychology buffs, incorrectly believe that simple means easy, that knowledge is the same as action, and that academic or textbook understanding and applied psychology are one and the same. "I've heard that before," or "I studied that in school" pressures the perfectionist to insist that he or she should not slip into emotional inefficiencies.

Some of my most difficult clients are those who have had previous therapy, or had a class or major in a human service curriculum. Many come away from such involvements with weak, once-over-lightly knowledge rather than a convincing understanding of what makes humans tick. Regardless of how well-versed one becomes in the intricacies of human behavior, emotional cavities of varying degrees will continue to prevail. The problem is that the perfectionist has difficulty accepting this. A former client insisted that because she had been in therapy for months and had solved several of her problems she "should" also be able to lose weight like she "had to." She discovered that putting excessive pressure on herself increased her tension level, which encouraged her to eat even more. Another illustration of the ultra-perfectionistic is the client who worked diligently at lightening her burden of self-inflicted guilt feelings, only to report that after overcoming her primary problem of guilt, she felt guilty for not feeling guilty.

By trying to do the impossible, perfectionistic drivers put a real strain on daily living and a definite damper on personal happiness. As one client said, "Oh, you mean lighten up on yourself without giving up on yourself." The following are some practical suggestions for closing the gap between utopian expectations and everyday realities.

1. *Admit the Problem.* See that it's not a question of whether or not you are a perfectionist, but to what extent this is so. Understanding this will give you an idea of how much work you have to do, and being open with yourself may provide some emotional relief in itself.
2. *Accept Yourself with the Problem.* Don't be hard on yourself for having this human trait. Not yet being able to accept your fallible nature does not diminish your value to yourself as a human being. You would be better off without the problem, but you wouldn't be a better person.
3. *Disputing Irrational Perfectionistic Ideas (Irrational Beliefs - IBs).* This is a primary technique of rational-emotive therapy (RET) and entails detecting, identifying, debating, and disputing the masochistic philosophical views that are at the core of emotional problems. Then, because RET is applied philosophy, one is encouraged to apply these new-found values and beliefs, cultivating a lifestyle that will reflect the acceptance that mental health stands for rather than the demandingness that per-

fectionism as emotional disturbance represents. Examples of creative self-disputing are:

- *IB*: "I must succeed and perform exceptionally well in this and all other important life tasks and challenges or I'll turn into an inferior being."

  Dispute: "Where is the evidence that I have to succeed and do exceptionally well in this or any other activity and that if I don't I'll turn into an inferior being?"

  Answer: "There is no evidence that I must succeed and do well at this or at anything else. Likewise, there is no proof that my failing would diminish me as a person. It is true that I want to do well and would probably find it very nice if I did succeed. In fact, because of all the advantages of displaying my capabilities, I'm going to work very determinedly to do just that. If I don't accomplish my goal I will feel disappointed and regretful, but I will choose not to rate myself as a second-class citizen for not succeeding."

- *IB*: "Others have to treat me fairly and kindly, agree with me, and otherwise patronize my values and way of thinking. When they don't, they deserve to be damned and rated as inconsiderate, subhuman, rotten individuals."

  Dispute: "Where is the law of the universe that states others are required to do well by me, treat me in a considerate, affirmative manner, and see things my way rather than have a mind of their own and treat me badly if they so choose?"

  Answer: "Although I like it better and it is more pleasant when others validate and support me, there is obviously no universal law that others are mandated to act or think in ways that I find comforting, approving, and pleasing."

- *IB*: "Life must make it easy for me to accomplish my goals, achieve my ends, and generally gain all that I want in what it has to offer. When this does not swiftly and efficiently occur, I'll whine, moan, withdraw, pity myself, and procrastinate so I can get even with life - even if it means cutting off my nose in spite of my face."

Dispute: "Demonstrate the proof that I am to be convenienced in gaining what I desire in life. Where does it say that it is essential that I bemoan my plight when advantages don't promptly and automatically befall me?"

Answer: "There is no proof that bears witness to my being given any special favors en route to striving for my goals in life. Furthermore, it is unwise to presume that listlessness, inertia, or shirking are required or beneficial reactions to the grim reality that life was apparently not made for me."

- *IB*: "I have to feel calm, cool, collected, and serene, and be in total control of my feelings at all times. It is awful and terrible, or intolerable and degrading, when I experience the emotional discomfort that I should, must, and ought not to experience."

Dispute: "What are the special reasons for my having to be in total control of my feelings? Why should I never feel anxious, nervous, shameful, depressed, guilty, fearful, angry, or jealous?"

Answer: "Because of my human limitations, just like everyone else, I have emotional tumors of varying proportions. Therefore, there are no special reasons why I must never experience emotional queasiness. It is true that I want and prefer to have a better handle on my emotions, but I can do that better when I accept myself rather than get caught up in denying the innate holes in my head."

● *IB*: "I am responsible for other people's problems and disturbances, and must direct their efforts toward a happy ending. Not seeking and finding a perfect solution to their unhappiness and misery means that I care for them less, and I have to feel guilty for not fulfilling my duty."

Dispute: "Where is the evidence that I am required to do other people's work for them in their happiness-seeking attempts? How does it show that I am less concerned and should feel guilty for not becoming consumed in others' misfortunes?"

Answer: "There are no universal dictates that say that I must try and solve others' problems for them, or that I am responsible for their unpleasant life conditions. Furthermore, I need not feel guilty when I choose not to take on the burdens of the world or individuals in it. It is true that I can consider the problems of individuals in my social group and do my best to offer assistance within my limits of time, energy, and resources when solicited to do so. Such contributions, when given in a flexible, well-thought-out manner, are really in my best interest because they may improve my ongoing association with these individuals."

● *IB*: "Life's decisions have to be made accurately, so when I come to a fork in the decision-making road, I have to know what choice will be best in the long-run. Until I know for sure, I'll ride the same decision-making fence. After all, to not be precisely on target in making the correct choice would be catastrophic, and would leave me unable to live with myself."

Dispute: "Why must I hit the bull's-eye or even come close to the mark in decision-making accuracy? In addition, why am I required to know tomorrow's answers today?

Why would it be the end of the world if I happened to be incorrect in my judgment?"

Answer: "It is true that making wrong choices is disappointing and may result in numerous personal inconveniences. However, there is no reason that I cannot make decisions based on present evidence, or that disaster and calamity would irreparably befall me in the face of wrong judgment. In fact, I could put lessons from such errors to use in upcoming decisions."

● *IB*: "I have to have the approval of and acceptance from all others that I deem significant. Not gaining this total liking is too much for me to bear. It not only prevents me from accepting myself, but in addition, makes me an unworthy human being."

Dispute: "While it is nice to be acknowledged, liked, and approved by important people in my life, it is not necessary to gain such positive recognition. Further, why would I have to reject myself and define myself as a substandard individual simply because others select against me?"

Answer: "There is no valid evidence that I require acceptance and approval from important others to live, survive, and find some degree of happiness in my life. While it is better to be well-thought-of by valued associates, there is no proof that because something is better I have to have it. In these important relationships I can do my best to be myself without trying desperately to prove myself. In that process I will probably gain as well as lose some social favor. When the latter results, that will be undelightful and sad but hardly tragic. By accepting myself I can sanely counter the pangs of hurt or disapproval anxiety."

Taking 10 to 15 minutes a day to forcefully review those antiperfectionistic ideas that apply to you will begin to lighten the perfectionistic load that blocks you from gaining more of the pleasure and less of the pain of daily living.

4. *Purposefully Court Mistakes.* The best way to change an irrational belief is to act against it. Intentionally do, say, think, and feel in ways that are off perfectionism's territory. Deliberately act like you have forgotten the day of the week, purposefully take a contrary view in social conversation, think in ways that you consider off-base, willfully create and escalate uncomfortable feelings you believe to be unacceptable. Follow these wrong turns in an innocent way that won't get you into legal problems or handicap you in a vital way, such as losing your job. Determine ahead of time that you are not going to down or otherwise upset yourself for your out-of-character actions. Intentionally doing what you normally forbid yourself to do will encourage the loosening of perfectionistic bents.

5. *Transparency.* Openly admit your mistakes to your peers several times daily. Taking pressure off yourself in not trying to conceal your obviously fallible nature is a way of accepting yourself, regardless of your performance.

6. *Coping Statements.* List several antiperfectionistic thoughts, carry these around with you, and repeat them strongly to yourself several times a day; or write them on notes and leave them in conspicuous places, such as on the refrigerator or the bathroom mirror, for your frequent review. When drilled persistently, these self-reminders and their rational messages may begin to take on special meaning and lead to your acting upon them. Such self-statements might include: "perfectionism paralyzes"; "give yourself some emotional slack"; "I have a right to be wrong"; "I can be myself, I don't have to prove myself"; "my best doesn't mean the best"; "lighten up"; "go easy."

7. *Referenting.* Calling to mind the advantages of flexibility and acceptance and the disadvantages of rigidity and ultimate exactness provides a basis for comparison. Writing these down and reviewing them provides a regular reminder of the value of thinking about and doing what's best in a nonperfectionistic way.

8. *Self and Other Validation Training.* Perfectionistic acting people frequently are overly critical, nit-picking, and faultfinding. Make a special point to seek out what is good in self, others, and life, and openly share what you discover. This is a practical way to counter the focus on the half-empty part of the bottle, a typical perfectionist tendency.

Perfectionism robs you of enjoyment, happiness, and fulfillment. It is like an invisible emotional straitjacket, demanding impossible expectations of self, others, and life. True personal development and happiness comes from simply accepting yourself, others, and life regardless. This won't bring about the best of all possible worlds, but will probably provide more of the good that life has to offer.

Note. From *Think Straight! Feel Great! 21 Guides to Emotional Self-Control* by Bill Borcherdt, ACSW, Copyright 1989, Professional Resource Exchange, Inc., P.O. Box 15560, Sarasota, FL 34277-1560.

Condemning the Sin But Not the Sinner: Overcoming the Odds Against Guilt

Whether it be about ill-advised behavior, uncalled-for thoughts, or unwanted feelings, humans possess strong tendencies to make themselves feel guilty. Additionally, more than other unwanted emotions, guilt tends to have a lingering, self-downing component. Unlike sorrow and regret, which sanely consist of a simple preference, wish, or desire that the mistake had not been made, guilt, in a perfectionistic, self-blaming way, advances those feelings beyond being associated with a wrong doing.

The idea that, "I wish I hadn't made that mistake; I'll try to correct my obvious error in the present and not make the same mistake again in the future" will motivate self-change, increasing the likelihood of future advantages and solutions. On the other hand, the notion that "I should not have committed this mistake, and because I did I should condemn and damn myself" will result in strong feelings of self-betrayal and self-belittlement, and block happiness-seeking goals. In short, guilt is when you violate or trespass your values and blame yourself for it.

Unfortunately, this fire-and-brimstone approach is often seen as the solution to correcting one's blunders and getting on with one's life in a way that will bring about more of the advantages and less of the disadvantages. In reality, this self-flagellation will more than likely end up to (a) be emotional hell on earth in the form of self-depreciation and resultant feelings of guilt, insecurity, and inferiority; and (b) perpetuate rather than correct the problems concerned. Condemning yourself because of your mistake, rather than accepting yourself in spite of it, will paradoxically result in multiplying and duplicating mistakes rather than correcting them. This guide will focus on minimizing the guilt habit while more efficiently getting the job done - correcting the act without damning the actor.

In an effort to turn down this self-imposed moral pressure cooker, let's look at some of the mistaken ideas that contribute to guilt as an emotional problem.

MISTAKEN IDEA NUMBER ONE

"Guilt gets positive results." Actually, productivity decreases in direct proportion to how guilty we feel. Movement toward corrective, constructive action is increasingly blocked the more upset we get with ourselves for goofing.

MISTAKEN IDEA NUMBER TWO

"Guilt is a normal, healthy emotion." This assumes that unless we down ourselves for our wrongdoing, we will continue to harm others in the future. On the contrary, we will have more energy for the benefit of our social group when we stop draining ourselves in self-recrimination. Feeling guilty may be normal because most people are not very compassionate with themselves after making a mistake. However, it is not healthy because of the mental anguish and unproductive behavior it creates.

MISTAKEN IDEA NUMBER THREE

"Being guilty is the same as feeling guilty." This overgeneralized notion has antihumanistic qualities by assuming that we have no choice in determining our feeling response to being in error. We could actually choose not to feel guilty following a goof. With this more clearheaded outlook comes a greater probability of picking and choosing from more constructive future alternatives. Outer problems in the form of poor choices are frequently escalated into inner problems by becoming bogged down in willful guilt and self-blame.

MISTAKEN IDEA NUMBER FOUR

"If you don't feel guilty for your mistake, you don't have any feelings at all." This all-or-nothing way of looking at our emotional response to our faults fails to see shades of gray at the feeling level. In fact, the more appropriate, moderate feelings of sadness, regret, and sorrow are more likely to encourage alternative, advantageous ways of dealing with the situation the next time around. With regret comes motivation to do better next time; with guilt, the primary incentive is to condemn oneself rather than correct the ill-advised behavior.

MISTAKEN IDEA NUMBER FIVE

"If you don't feel guilty, you're an immoral person." The opposite is actually true, because it is immoral to hurt a human being, including yourself, and when you make yourself feel guilty as opposed to regretful, you harm yourself.

MISTAKEN IDEA NUMBER SIX

"When you wrong, frustrate, deprive, or inconvenience someone and don't feel guilty about it, you do not love or otherwise care about that individual and his or her well-being." Emotional suffering that you may cause yourself following neglect of your associate has got nothing to do with your fondness for that person. Harming yourself after the neglect only proves that you can give yourself two problems for the price of one.

MISTAKEN IDEA NUMBER SEVEN

"People who are guilty of doing something wrong are bad people who should be looked down upon and ostracized." The idea that people are the same as their behavior sets the guilt cycle in motion. People do their behavior, but they are not their behavior. To think otherwise leads to self-blame when you do the wrong thing and other-blame when your companion is in violation.

MISTAKEN IDEA NUMBER EIGHT

"If you don't feel guilty about anything, you don't value anything." Because you stubbornly refuse to damn yourself for falling short of the mark does not mean that you do not cherish your goals. It means that you value yourself enough not to emotionally harm yourself for not realizing and achieving what you believed was important enough to try to accomplish.

MISTAKEN IDEA NUMBER NINE

"Solutions to problems of feeling guilty are practical and pragmatic rather than philosophical." The belief in penance and atonement as the path to the unguilty promised land is a misconception often leading to frantic, self-sacrificing behaviors. Such self-cleansing actions are unnecessary, and are usually done in desperation to ward off flooding feelings of guilt and fear of impending damnation. Your appetite for such overcompensating behavior can be insatiable, with the self-doubting question becoming "How much is enough?"

To counter this tendency begin by challenging your irrational belief system that created the guilt, and then forgive yourself for exercising your right to be wrong. You may choose to gracefully apologize and in some way make amends for your goof, demonstrating sincere regret for your negative act. However, such strivings are better done for self-choosing rather than compulsive reasons. Simply stating, "I'm sorry, and I regret any harm or inconvenience I may have created for you; I plan on doing better in the future" serves its purpose better than overapologizing or degrading yourself.

MISTAKEN IDEA NUMBER TEN

"If you don't feel guilty you *should* feel guilty, and if you do feel guilty you shouldn't feel guilty." This double-barreled demand leaves you damned if you do and damned if you don't, never quite resolving your guilt complex. In the first case, you wrongly believe that you are mandated to be hard on yourself. In the second case, because you think you have to be perfect at not falling off the guilt-avoidance wagon, you give yourself a double whammy - feeling guilty about your feeling guilty.

MISTAKEN IDEA NUMBER ELEVEN

"In some situations you ought to feel guilty for doing the right thing or guilty for doing the wrong thing." This is another one of those double-bind, no-win situations in which you can allow yourself to get caught. For instance, if you rightly act in your self-interest and say "no" to a friend's or child's request, but wrongly believe that friendship or parenting goes hand in hand with obligation or agreement, you are likely to feel guilty. Likewise, if you wrongly abide by a friend or your child's request and rigidly think you are not entitled to use poor judgment, the same feelings of guilt will result.

MISTAKEN IDEA NUMBER TWELVE

"Wrong actions, mistakes, errors, and shortcomings cause guilt." It is your evaluation of the misdeed, not the act itself, that creates feelings of guilt. More precisely, your absolute insistence that you not be wrong, and the accompanying negative self-evaluation as it ties into your error, determines the guilt. Give up the demand for rightness and the drive for righteousness with its inevitable self-blame, and you will put a dent in the guilt habit.

Guilt is a special form of anxiety that is extremely harsh and disabling. The following practical suggestions are aimed at countering these mistaken ideas by taking definitive action against guilt:

1. Clearly understand that your mistaken act does not make you feel guilty, but rather the faulty processing of your behavior through your belief system. Acknowledge and challenge these philosophical distortions and see if you don't get better-feeling results. Instead of assuming, "I should not have been wrong," ask yourself, "Do not I, like all human beings, have a right to be wrong?" Rather than telling yourself, "How awful and horrible that I was wrong," self-state "Being wrong may not have been the best thing for me to be, but why is being wrong so horrendous and such a disaster?" "I can learn from my mistake and, if nothing else, use it as a stepping stone to become more tolerant and accepting of myself."

2. Have some innocent fun with your tendency to take your fallible nature too seriously by purposefully making mistakes, such as going down an elevator looking to the rear, taking a controversial stand on a public issue, going down the wrong aisle in a theatre, or asking what time it is - a.m. or p.m. Make up your mind ahead of time that you are not going to

damn yourself for these behaviors, while convincing yourself that you're not an ass for acting asininely.

3. Write on a fill-in-the-blank note card "I forgive myself for (whatever mistake you made) because (list reasons for self-forgiveness)." After identifying your mistakes and listing reasons to forgive yourself for making them (e.g., "I'm only human; life is too short not to; I have a right to be wrong"), put the card on your bathroom mirror and read it while you're brushing your teeth in the morning so you can start the day off rationally. Then, carry the card during the day and review it, preferably out loud to yourself, several times a day until you strongly convince yourself of its rational message.

4. Use transparency, self-disclosure assignments - Purposefully reveal to associates mistakes you have made while indicating your intention to do better in the future. Starting with: "I never told anybody this before . . ." will especially help to pressure yourself less about past mistakes, which will also help pave the way to making fewer errors in the future.

5. Imagine what good advice you would give a friend who made mistakes similar to yours, and give yourself that same good advice.

6. Vividly picture yourself erring, but push yourself to not feel guilty in your imagined wrongdoing.

7. Watch your choice of words. Be more precise in your descriptions of your faults. Minimize one liners that exaggerate and overgeneralize, such as, "I *never* do it right"; "I'm *always* wrong"; "*Every time* I try I fail." Such language abuse promotes a hopeless view of life that says corrections cannot be made by a person who is never changing.

8. Call to mind, focus on, and affirm what you've done right, and purposefully blow up the pleasant, satisfying feelings about what you have mastered.

9. Project into time by asking yourself if your mistake is going to be such a big deal weeks, months, or years from now.
10. Redefine a wrong decision or a judgment call as a position made on present evidence.
11. Role-play with yourself by writing, "I am a human who forgives himself or herself by _____": for example, "being self-compassionate"; "taking risks and sometimes floundering but seldom blaming myself for it"; "seeing and accepting myself as a total person who is bigger than any of my traits"; "finding value in myself by myself"; and so on. Then read your essay daily, and during the next week try to become the self-forgiving person you would like to become.
12. Don't give yourself symptom stress by insisting that you never feel guilty. When you upset yourself about having the problem, you will not be able to work as well at giving up the problem. It would be better to self-state "All right, so I'm making myself feel guilty. How can I rid myself of this unpleasant feeling without being hard on myself for creating it?"

Guilt frequently starts by doing the wrong thing for the right reasons, or good intentions gone awry. This is followed by attempts to compensate and atone for mistakes by doing the right thing for the wrong reason, for the purpose of changing oneself from a bad person to a good person. Completing the cycle of overcoming guilt comes with doing the right thing for the right reason: correct your mistake not for self-enhancement, but to experience more of the advantages and joys and less of the disadvantages and hassles of everyday life.

Winning out over guilt leanings has three advantages: (a) you will experience more personal happiness more often; (b) you can greatly increase the probability of attaining more of life's benefits; and (c) you will be less likely to hold yourself back from achieving future goals. Such preferable outcomes may not result in perpetual satisfaction, but may improve your general sense of well-being, from which a more meaningful, self-actualized lifestyle can flow. Replace your self-condemning, invisible emotional straitjacket with a more self-forgiving, emotionally liberated life jacket, and discover the life- and happiness-saving results for yourself!

Note. From *Think Straight! Feel Great! 21 Guides to Emotional Self-Control* by Bill Borcherdt, ACSW, Copyright 1989, Professional Resource Exchange, Inc., P.O. Box 15560, Sarasota, FL 34277-1560.

Ask Me No Questions and
I'll Tell You No Lies:
Roots of Deceitfulness

"Liar, liar, your pants are on fire - your nose is as long as a telephone wire." Like the fairy tale character Pinocchio, whose nose continued to lengthen with each dishonest statement, it is difficult to understand why individuals lie as often as they do, particularly when it often gets them into hot water with their social or family group. Whether it be a child who insists that black is white and white is black, or a colleague, friend, or other associate who perpetually lies, such over- or mis-statements are at best frustrating, perplexing, and most difficult to reckon with. This guide gives a range of possible explanations for the counterproductive behavior of chronic or frequent lying; and explains what can be done to protect oneself and deal more effectively with such frustrating, annoying antics. It describes in detail the problems of associating with an untrustworthy acting person and provides guidelines for effectively and efficiently dealing with such a person.

The following are possible, not so obvious motivations for purposeful deceitful behavior:

1. *Low Frustration Tolerance (LFT).* Avoiding the exaggerated negative consequences, the pain that may come from telling the truth, promotes

the falsification of reality. The primary demand is: "I shouldn't have to suffer the natural consequences of my mistaken behavior"; and/or "It would be unbearable if these consequences were to befall me, so I'll avoid what must not happen and what would devastate me if it did." Unpleasantness *can* result from one's errors. However, low frustration tolerance dramatizes the negative consequences of owning up to one's actions.

I can think of two separate clients who mismanaged and diverted others' funds, only to try desperately to cover their financial tracks. At the core of the escalation of their illegal activity was the irrational notion that the immediate consequences of admitting their mistake were just too much to bear; in panic, they ended up multiplying the original misdeed. A rush of emotional relief was gained immediately when a decision was made to hold off revealing the financial misdealings; the problem then snowballed further, so that the eventual consequences were even harsher.

Another accompanying demand to LFT says: "I shouldn't have to do what I don't want to do, and if I were forced to I couldn't stand it, so I'll lie with a straight face to avoid that outcome." The predetermined, imagined, horrendous consequences of the required chore lead to fooling oneself about the difficulty of the task, which leads to fooling others to avoid what has been blown up to be the ultimate in pain.

2. *Ego Anxiety.* A secondary demand that "I must perform perfectly and gain the total approval of all those I associate with, or else I'm perfectly worthless" is another primary reason for choosing to lie. To get others to respond with awe can be a temporary ego massage sometimes gained by stretching the truth, but feelings of insecurity can be only temporarily allayed by making the unbelievable seem believable.

3. *Anger and Revenge.* Pulling another's leg is frequently used as an excuse or justification for telling falsehoods, sometimes motivated by a desire to get even for felt injustices. Then, after being caught in the lie and confronted with it, the rationalization can be given, "I'm glad I lied as upset as he was with me." Behind avenging motives is the irrational belief that "others must not do wrong by me, and when they do they deserve to be damned and punished as rotten individuals." In other words, "It's natural that I lie and deceive such evil people; they have it coming anyway."

4. *Excitement-Seeking Tendencies.* One way to spice up an otherwise boring existence is to lay theatrical claim to experiences and knowledge that most mere mortals never have.

5. *Dire Need for Control.* Sometimes a sure-fire way to get others to respond to your wishes is to work on their suggestibility and vulnerability. Taking such unfair advantage can provide a feeling of power and control, dictating the structure of the other's response by the use of falsehoods. Taking away another's freedom of choice and action can sometimes create the grandiose feelings that go along with the illusion of universal control.

6. *Disapproval Anxiety.* The idea that one would melt in the face of others' disapproval can be the driving force behind dishonesty. After all, if "others' opinions equal me," then I had better preserve my essence by only saying what I think others want to hear.

7. *Conflict Anxiety.* When conflict is seen as unbearable, it is to be avoided at all costs, including wearing a mask at the risk of losing face when it is taken off or using lies in an effort to avoid such a perceived calamity.

8. *Shame.* Shame begets deceitfulness when public disclosure of faults and shortcomings seems more than one can bear, thus making it convenient to falsify facts. If scorn and ridicule are seen as self-diminishing, perceived self-

value is increased by stacking the deck in favor of others' positive opinions.

9. *Fear of Failure.* Rationalizing or blatantly denying mistakes frequently is used to cover-up
the horror of being wrong and keep perfectionistic bents in business.

10. *Deprivation Anxiety.* Overfocusing on the essen-
tialness of reaching one's goals encourages
deceit in an effort to control the conditions of
life to meet these self-made demands.

11. *Fear of Rejection.* Social deceptions told about
oneself can be used as protective devices to:
(a) keep people at a distance, for fear that if
they found out what you were really like they
would despise you; and (b) avoid coming to
terms with your loneliness by believing that if
you really decided to honestly open up, such
transparency would make you irresistible in
the eyes of others, but that such self-disclosure
"just isn't me."

The following guidelines can be followed in
one's relationship with a person who, for whatever
reason(s), speaks with a forked tongue:

1. *Don't Personalize the Other's Problem.* Avoid
feeling hurt by not assuming that his or her
dishonesty is a reflection on you - you just happened to be the target.

2. *Don't Damn Him or Her.* Avoid making yourself angry and seeking vengeance. Instead, try
and see his or her trickery as a reflection of
human being limitations and as just one part
of the total individual. Take a balanced view
of the person and focus on some of his or her
more desirable characteristics.

3. *Avoid "Cornering."* Don't get involved in verbal
manipulation, attempting to catch him or her
in a lie by asking questions to which you already know the answer. This is a form of deceitfulness itself, and contributes to perpetuating the problem you would like to correct.

4. *Level with Him or Her.* Make a firm, direct statement about what the dishonesty means for you, incorporating the following: (a) Start by affirming those parts of the relationship you appreciate and hope will continue. (b) Be crystal clear about your feelings of betrayal, annoyance, and irritation, as well as personal inconveniences caused by his or her untruths. (c) Explain that you would like help with your problems that stem from the dishonesty, and solicit his or her help with these difficulties. For example, "There are many parts of our relationship that I do appreciate and I would like to be able to appreciate it even more. Here is how I think I can do that. I get concerned and feel sad and deceived when not told the truth. Therefore, I would like you to help by being honest with me in the future so that I can enjoy our association even more. Are you willing to help me with this?" This approach to diplomatic emotional self-control does not assure good results, but does increase the likelihood of success more than the angry, finger-pointing alternative.

5. *Don't Get Derailed.* Stay on the target subject even if the deceiver attempts to deny, diminish, counter, or in some other way avoid the issue. If necessary, become a broken record in stating and restating your concerns and potential solutions to your disenchantment.

6. *Restate Your Concerns and Objectives.* If the sender does not take his or her cue from your original position, a reasonable amount of reminding may be in order. When you become aware of continued lying, you can reflect back on your beginning position and once again request that he or she refrain from such antics. Along with this, refuse to discuss the matter further. Explain that while you are not willing to continue talking about the deceit, you are willing to discuss other matters openly and honestly.

7. *Offer to Help.* Rather than trying to give unsolicited advice, attempt to get the green light in advising more rational views. Understand that the following key irrational beliefs make it convenient to lie:

- "I can't stand negative consequences."
- "I must impress others and gain their approval."
- "Others don't have a right to be wrong and I have to get even when they are."
- "Boredom is awful and I have to have excitement even if it is contrived."
- "Conflict is terrible and to be avoided at all costs."
- "Undressing my faults is shameful, and instead they must always be concealed."
- "I must not be deprived of what I want."
- "Others' rejection is devastating."

Encourage your peer to identify, challenge, and uproot these mistaken notions. Otherwise the problem is likely to persist.
8. *Define Conditions and Consequences.* If lack of cooperation consistently recurs, more concrete measures may be in order. Specifically, state that a condition of this relationship is mutual trust, without which there can be no relationship. If some measure of control exists in the relationship, you can make it clear in a firm, nondamning way how you will make it uncomfortable each time the other behaves dishonestly.
9. *Leave the Door Open.* If the other party continues to manufacture falsehoods, express your regrets for the present state of the relationship and withdraw or considerably curtail your involvement. It is probably not worth the frustration for you and may be reinforcing the other person's lack of responsibility in a relationship. Let it be known that you would be willing to continue the involvement at a future date if forthrightness and trust were the rule

rather than the exception. Although honesty may not be the only policy, it is likely to be the best one if the mutual goal is to establish legitimate, open lines of communication.

Note. From *Think Straight! Feel Great! 21 Guides to Emotional Self-Control* by Bill Borcherdt, ACSW, Copyright 1989, Professional Resource Exchange, Inc., P.O. Box 15560, Sarasota, FL 34277-1560.

Survival Skills for Protecting Yourself From a Difficult-Acting Person

When a disturbed, emotionally upset, or antagonistic acting individual is intent on making his or her problems your problems, you have a number of self-protective alternatives for temporarily distancing yourself from the other's spiteful intentions. Dealing with such a harassing individual is not easy, but it can be done in a way that will better insure your own emotional and physical well-being. This guide pinpoints some of the attitude and behavior alternatives available to prevent your getting caught up in someone else's problems and disturbances.

Before detailing the range of positive possibilities when you begin to feel yourself under the gun, these "how not to do it" responses are best to keep in mind:

- Don't deny the allegation or the other's account of your shortcomings.
- Don't get defensive and think you have to spell out and prove your goodness and the badness of what was spewed your way.
- Don't counterattack by aggressively bad mouthing your attacker.

- Don't overexplain or make any effort to convince your tormentor of something he or she doesn't want to be convinced of.
- Don't apologize for something that may not have been your fault or responsibility to begin with.
- Don't justify yourself and your existence in a humble, atoning way.

Embarking on any or all of these above actions is likely to prove frustrating. No matter what you say, it is probably not what he or she wants to hear anyway, and you will simply paint yourself into a corner. Furthermore, such self-defeating actions will encourage your predator to think you and your emotions are at his or her mercy. What *to do* in response to such problematic circumstances rests on the following two beliefs:

1. *Others Have a Right to Be Wrong.* Strongly *convince* yourself that, as much as you may not like it, other people have a right to act in contrary ways. Though they may be wrong, and though it might be better if they didn't act badly, to demand that they not exercise their right to do the wrong thing is to insist that they not be human, but instead be superhuman. Fully acknowledging and accepting this human given allows you to better control your emotional response to the other's ill-advised behavior.

2. *Accept Yourself.* Once you strongly believe that the other's bad behavior toward you or negative criticism of you does *not* equal you, you are protected emotionally from his or her wrath. As Eleanore Roosevelt said, "Nobody can make you feel inferior unless you give them permission." By emotionally distancing yourself and refusing to take an unkind comment and turn it into an insult, you are shielding yourself from psychological hurt. Nobody can magically get into your gut and cause you emotional pain; only your personalized response can do that. From this emotionally

self-sufficient stance you will be able to use the practical behavioral tools suggested below:

- *Become an echo.* Use yourself as a sounding board for the feeling part of the other person's response to you. Going beyond the content of the issues that are adversely presented to the feelings behind them will often defuse and neutralize the sender's negative feelings. It is difficult to remain hostile to someone who empathically responds to the feeling rather than the content of what is said. "You sound angry"; "It sounds like you have really got a problem with that"; "That seems to really meet with your disapproval" are all examples of this type of empathy training.
- *Find some truth to what the other person is saying.* No matter what anyone says about you, there is always some truth to it. Locate that part of the negative message that is true and reflect it back to the sender. Thus, if someone says, "You're a lousy dresser," you can respond with, "Sometimes I do dress badly." If told, "You're a real lousy person," you can return with, "Sometimes I do act badly." Use qualifying words such as "sometimes," "maybe," and "possibly" that allow partial agreement, however minute. This has the net effect of putting up a smoke screen, making it difficult for the verbal attacker to pursue further. Also, it is difficult to harass someone who finds some validity in what is said.
- *Ask a question about the sender's negative criticisms.* Asking for detailed particulars about negative commentary directed toward you makes the sender more accountable and responsible for what he or she is saying. It forces him or her to cough up documentation for his or her position. No one likes to be put on the spot when attempting to exploit others' vulnerabilities, so this request may be

all it takes to encourage your adversary to think twice before directing unkind comments toward you in the future. "What is it about my dress that you don't like?"; "What is it about my behavior that you find objectionable?"; "What specifically about my job performance do you find unmeritorious?" are all examples of soliciting precision while discouraging such unpleasantries in the future. This approach also allows you to develop emotional immunity to others' criticisms by actively seeking out precisely what others are negatively saying.

- *Agree.* When the other's criticisms are on target, both in kind and degree, openly admit your mistake or acknowledge your fault. Applaud your humanness by verifying the correctness of what is being critically said about you. Thus, if you're accurately told "That was a stupid mistake," celebrate your shortcoming with "You're right - that was a stupid mistake! I plan on doing better next time." Strongly agreeing with a valid criticism is an indication of emotional stability that accepts the limits of human fallibility in a nondefensive, fully self-accepting way.

- *"I" statements.* Making a position statement of your convictions and your feelings about your convictions is a form of responsible self-expression that encourages people to listen more attentively. "I disagree"; "I don't like what you just said"; "I still have value to myself, no matter what you say or do"; "I want to think about it"; "I don't want or need that" are all examples of firm, controlled responses that come from a position of strength and potency.

- *Say nothing.* There is no universal law that you have to respond to someone who is trying to give you a hard time. Because someone is making a statement or asking you a question designed to emotionally manipulate and intimidate you doesn't mean you have to respond in the way he or she wants. If you instead distract yourself and become a solemn broken record in the face of his or her barbs, your harasser will likely become discouraged and frustrated, and therefore unlikely to repeat the performance.

- *Offer selective silence.* Let the other person know that you are willing to converse with him or her about certain issues, but *not* those about which he or she is upset. This permits you to respond only to topics you think are advantageous to discuss, and avoid those that may fuel up the emotional fires. "I'm not willing to continue our conversation about this matter because I feel we will just end up yelling and fighting, but I am willing to talk about other matters after things get calmed down"; followed by silence, this is an effective tool to prevent yourself from getting caught up in someone else's obnoxious behavior.

- *Take a time out.* If your aggressor continues to pursue you even when you avoid answering his or her third-degree questions and emotionally charged statements, remove yourself from his or her presence. Go to another room, take a walk, or engage in some other activity both to discourage him or her and to nullify your reaction to the continued harassment. Detaching yourself by physically exiting from his or her presence temporarily protects you from the contrary behavior, while driving home the message that there are limits to how long you are willing to put up with this behavior.

- *When all else fails.* If you have exercised all of the previous sensible alternatives and your nemesis continues to emotionally stalk you, it is time to accept that you have an out-of-control child, seriously disturbed mate, or hopelessly temperamental friend or companion on your hands. You would do well to set limits with such an emotionally unsettled individual, lest you risk continued verbal, and possibly physical, abuse. In the case of the child, seek out the back-up of the juvenile officer; with the mate who won't change, consulting with a divorce lawyer or abuse shelter may be the only option; with nonfamily members who insist on violating your rights to privacy and protection from abuse, it might be advisable to get a legal restraining order and insist on police enforcement.

Putting your self-protection first while utilizing one or a combination of the previous options frees you to pursue your personal happiness in more flexible, well-thought-out, unobstructed ways.

Note. From *Think Straight! Feel Great! 21 Guides to Emotional Self-Control* by Bill Borcherdt, ACSW, Copyright 1989, Professional Resource Exchange, Inc., P.O. Box 15560, Sarasota, FL 34277-1560.

Emotional Dependency, Fear, and Anger: Killing Three Birds with One Stone

"You only hurt the ones you love" might be more accurately put, "You only fear the ones you hate." One of the rare, sane commercialized love songs said: "Got along without you before I met you, I am going to get along without you now." Perhaps an explanation for the contrasting statements is in order.

We mainly get angry at people we depend on. When others don't deliver what we think we require from them, anger frequently follows. The anger is both a disguise and an attempt to manipulate and control, camouflaging our fear of losing what appears mandatory for our emotional survival. It is also an attempt to intimidate the other person into supplying what we believe we desperately need from them. The possibility of losing that lifeline can appear awesome and devastating, with fear and anger creating emotional turmoil as we end up alternately fretting and resenting those who we think are our puppet masters. If I make myself emotionally dependent on you, and if you do not deliver what I feel I require, the logical conclusion is, "You deprived and hurt me, and you therefore deserve to be blamed and condemned as a rotten, wicked, individual - until the day you die - and I hope it's soon!"

We fear and resent others for what they might not do for us and for what we think or assume they can do to us. Viewing fear and anger as two peas in the emotional dependency pod allows us to more efficiently fine tune our emotions. Gains within gains are achieved with this triggering effect: knock off the emotional dependency and the fear and anger will also fall. This domino theory of emotional self-control abolishes the root of fear and anger by shooting down the emotional dependency that creates them. After all, if I no longer view you as my life raft to the promised land, I have less to lose and can begin to compensate for anything that you may deprive me of. When I see that my emotional survival is not on the line, what is there really to be fearful or angry about? As I become more emotionally self-reliant and self-sufficient, what basis is there left for emotional consumption? Furthermore, what advantages might become available from giving myself this emotional slack?

The following six questions concerning dependency will be answered in the remainder of this guide: What is emotional dependency? What are some of its dimensions? What are some of the causes of it? What are the disadvantages of getting caught up in it? What are the advantages of avoiding it? What are some strategies for avoiding its pitfalls?

1. Emotional dependency in a broader sense can include excessive reliance on fame, money, success, self-image, or even on being independent, to name a few. Within an RET context, emotional dependency in an interpersonal sense is a near total reliance on somebody to think, act, and feel toward you in a way that you believe is a requirement for your happiness and survival. You make yourself addicted to and begin to demand such essential, preferential treatment and feel lost without your relationship fix. The dependent person makes himself or herself emotionally paralyzed by his or her

demands for relationship certainty and begins to suffocate others, as well, ultimately sabotaging these all-consuming "needs" by driving others away. He or she doesn't ask, "Who needs a needy person?" and doesn't realize that the only thing he or she really needs is not to be needy.

2. Emotional dependency on another person takes various forms:

- *The need for undying, never-ending love and care.* The human leaning to bond with or attach to one another is an important part of what makes the world go around, but the demand for reciprocity - a return on one's emotional investment - can create utter frustration. The idea that if I rely on you, then you are obligated to respond to me with the same degree of emotional intensity, results in attempting the impossible: to control another human being. Feelings of hurt that may be created by another's perceived neglect quickly become anger when the following self-sentence is put into gear: "You hurt me, you bastard!" ("Because you didn't provide me with what I have to have from you.")
- *The need for never-questioning liking and approval.* The dependent's goal is to please another to the extent that he or she strives to be beyond reproach. When the dire need for approval is eventually shaken by not being able to please all of the people all of the time, fear and anger arise.
- *Requirements for unquestioning understanding.* The message becomes: "If you love me you will always understand me, and if you thwart me with your inability to always get inside my head and understand my logic, I'll act annoyed and irritated until you fulfill my reliance on you for 100% pure empathy and understanding" ("After all, that's the least you can do").

- *The need for kindness, friendliness, consideration, and favoritism.* Any lapses in the above
  will mean, "Since I am obviously not one of
  your favorite people any more, you are no
  longer one of mine." Individuals who make
  themselves dependent on significant others
  become very hard to live with when their
  demands are frustrated.

- *Insistence on fairness and eminent justice.* The
  idea that the world and everyone in it re-
  volves around me is age-appropriate for a 2-
  year-old, but in adults it shows marked imma-
  turity. The person dependent on "right is
  right" treatment doesn't stop to think that
  frequently what is right or wrong depends on
  whether you're asking or giving. To insist on
  something that doesn't exist - fairness and its
  derivatives of eminent justice - is to cook
  your own emotional goose. Ideas such as "the
  world was made for me," and "I'm the one
  person in the universe who has to always get
  what I deserve," creates dependency on illusory universal fairness.

- *The need for full-fledged, totally abiding acceptance.* Relying on unrelenting and unconditional acceptance is asking a lot. People
  are different and tend to shun those who do
  not share and accept their values, traits, and
  ways of being. As with the other dependen-
  cies, fear and anger will result from the philosophical requirement for total acceptance.

- *The need for agreement.* The demand to "see
  eye to eye with me" to meet my emotional desires creates mixed anguish and hatred when
  ultimate compatibility doesn't happen.

- *The need for validation, affirmation, and
  praise.* This view states that "I need to have
  you acknowledge, recognize, and praise my
  special talent, skill, or good deed, or nurture
  me for no special reason." Disappointment
  and bitterness result when such demands
  aren't always met.

- *The need for repeated cooperation.* Insistence upon forever seeing and doing things my way results in a high level of resentment when these wishes aren't met.
- *The need for the presence of another person.* Depending on someone else to always be around leaves a void of displeasure when he or she is unavailable.

3. Some core causes of emotional dependency include:

- *Ego reasons.* At the root of emotional dependency ties is the mistaken notion that "I have to gain from you certain favoritism and plaudits or else I'm somehow diminished as a human being." Approval and acceptance are made the sacred mainstay of one's emotional life.
- *Low Frustration Tolerance (LFT).* Agonizing about the absolute horror of going without someone else's presence or personal advantages leads to an anguishingly dependent state of mind. Giving excessive value to someone else's place in your life in the form of "I can't live without you"; "Being alone is awful"; "I need your love all the time" self-statements creates draining emotions that feed off these dependency demands.
- *Disapproval anxiety.* Worrying about others' possibly misunderstanding or disapproving of you creates emotional clinging that cements counterproductive dependency ties.
- *Conflict anxiety.* Creating a high stress level when facing potential differences of opinion creates an unrealistic obligation to agree at all times.
- *Perfectionism.* Refusal to live in a relationship world that is far less than perfect results from rigid insistence that all must be well all the time.
- *Genetic tendencies to bond and attach.* The basic human striving to attach and bond to

others is highly desirable, but demanding a return attachment causes problems. Because I attach myself to you, you must respond in kind - lest I despise and resent you for eternity. This immature thinking pattern states: "If I slobber all over you, you are mandated to do the same, and if you don't I'll hate myself for being deficient in my involvement efforts and/or loathe you because of your neglect."

4. The disadvantages of emotional dependency include the following:

- Like any addiction, emotional dependency has withdrawal symptoms in the form of mixed depression, hurt, fear, and anger. When abruptly deprived of mandatory emotional ties, alternate unwanted emotional responses are created in the absence of the relationship fix.
- Emotional dependency backfires by driving off those on whom you make yourself dependent. Others feel suffocated and view you as not much fun to be around due to your sense of urgency and desperation. Attempting to control another person only builds walls rather than bridges.
- Emotional dependency increases the likelihood of failure. Two sure ways to fail are to try and please everybody or to be petrified by the possibility of failing. Fear of failing at establishing close emotional ties and futile efforts to please other people produce a relationship-building style that makes you about as lovable as a wet mop.
- Heightened anxiety and tension levels follow from worrying about the possibility of one's relationship lifeline being cut. A dependent person frequently catastrophizes about losing what is viewed as one of life's prerequisites, and not getting it leaves him or her groping for emotional survival.

- Self-downing follows the irrational belief that "I'm nothing without _____." An emotionally clinging person typically feels he or she must control for these "needs" and sees failure as degrading when he or she cannot cope effectively with deprivation.

5. Some of the advantages of opting for more self-reliant, self-sufficient ways of living while avoiding dependency traps are:

- The less dependent person is minimally beholding to others and can be more honest, open, and direct in relationships with them. If you believe that you are not diminished in the face of dislike, you can more easily confront issues of concern in an above-board, free-wheeling manner.
- A self-reliant person is more fun to be around. By not relying on hidden agendas or requiring perpetual approval from others, you can afford to be more informal, casual, and fun-loving, less programmed, stressed, and tight-vested, and more accessible and appealing to others.
- Emotional emancipation encourages a more active-directive, experimenting, risk-taking approach to life that can greatly increase the likelihood of new personal discoveries. Such multiple experiences can contribute greatly to a well-rounded personality.
- Less grimness, and more joy and aliveness flow from worrying less about controlling for presumed essentials. Experiential benefits also flow from the emotional liberation of being more your own person.
- Greater problem-solving ability is often a side benefit of breaking the chains of dependency. Clearheadedness becomes the rule rather than the exception as the all-or-nothing thinking of the dependent individual is replaced by more flexible thought patterns.

- The less emotionally dependent you become, the more loving you are likely to be. No longer will you be mainly consumed with gaining love to prove yourself. As a result, you will be better able to give love; you will now understand that your life, manhood, or femininity does not rely on gaining what you viewed up until now as your love essentials. In giving love you are also more likely to get it in return.

6. Life is for learning, so experiment with some of the following suggestions for forcefully countering your emotionally dependent leanings:

   - *Create your own pleasures.* Take the initiative to develop pleasures suitable for you, incorporating a good number of possibilities that would require no one's cooperation but your own. The best way to change a faulty idea is to act against it, so prepare yourself for action by listing potential self-enjoying alternatives. Then, organize efforts to participate in those on the inventory that you have prioritized. Such self-concerted action will give you data that will disprove your original hypothesis that "I have to be hovered over or be with somebody to enjoy or find meaning to life."
   - *Learn to appreciate being alone.* Distinguish between being alone and being lonesome, and see that one doesn't have to lead to the other. Understand that much can be learned and appreciated with solitude. When in the company of yourself, concentrate on what you're doing and not on doing it alone, while keeping an eye on the advantages of going solo. For instance, a gourmet meal can often be experienced at a finer level when you can concentrate on every morsel rather than be distracted by company, however pleasant. Occasionally force yourself to stay alone and

enjoy yourself, especially at times such as weekends when you tend to be more inclined to rely on others for company and comfort.

- *Purposefully court disapproval.* Go out of your way to have innocent fun in setting yourself up for distain and disapproval from others. Say and do things that might bring a displeasurable response from your social group. Introduce ideas that may run counter to group discussion boundaries; purposefully make mistakes that will likely bring negative attention to you; appear in manner and dress that would be considered out of the ordinary in your associates' presence. This can behaviorally dispute your here-to-fore dependent tendencies on others' total liking and approval.

- *No self-blame.* Make it a strong point to not look down on yourself for being alone or when faced with other's disregard. Self-downingness in the face of adversity serves the self-defeating purpose of verifying your dependency on the objectionable circumstance or person.

- *Encourage independence in others.* Especially with those you depend on excessively, encourage a different pattern of relating. Discourage others from indulging your short-range dependency comfort to the neglect of your long-range self-development. Solicit their help by openly explaining your bondage problem and your desire to wean yourself from this other-directed pattern. Express your appreciation for their willingness to try to help you to sink, swim, or float on your own. Encourage their unavailability; get them to see that one of the kindest things they can do for you is to not make it too easy to depend on them for availability, cooperation, or any of your other desires and wants. One of the most loving things they can do for you is to expect more of you than you might otherwise expect of yourself.

- *Seek out independent models and associates.* Keep company with those who are pretty good at the self-striving skills that you wish to master. Ask them directly the secret of their success to assist you in fine tuning your own plans.
- *See yourself as inner-directed.* It is very difficult to become more the way you would like to become without imagining yourself that way. Plant pictures in your head that will better facilitate your plan to become more self-reliant.
- *Practice rational-emotive imagery.* First picture yourself in a circumstance where you tend to feel dependent, anxious, or fearful; next, force yourself to actually feel that discomfort as if you were there; last, continue imagining the same circumstance while changing these same fretful feelings to a healthy sense of concern, regret, or keen apprehensiveness. Practice this exercise once or twice a day, 5 to 10 minutes at a clip, and see if you can gain better control of unwanted emotions that offshoot from dependency. By practicing changing your feelings ahead of time, when you arrive at the moment of truth you are likely to be better able to produce feelings that will turn your dependency alarm down while mobilizing desired independence.
- *Keep in mind the benefits.* Itemize and then enlarge the pleasant feelings, thoughts, and images that accompany this more free-willed, spirited state. Escalating these very real advantages permits you to more fully appreciate this phase of your self-development.
- *Realign your attitudes.* Ask yourself, "What do I really need to survive?" "Why can't I tolerate disfavor?" "Why am I diminished as a person when others select against me?" "Why am I required to maintain a cooperative, nonconflictual relationship with those I deem significant, and why is it awful when I am unable

to do so?" These and other questions that dispute dependent-producing feelings of fear and anger will further encourage your independence.

- *Use strong coping statements.* Forcefully thinking thoughts that will better trigger independent action can be a powerful self-influence. How you talk to yourself can better promote self-interested behavior. Brief ideas such as "I always have myself; being alone doesn't mean being lonely"; "Tough if I'm not accepted"; "Cooperation and understanding are nice but not necessary" are examples of cue phrases that promote a more independent state of mind.

- *Affirmative conversation monitoring.* Contract with yourself to bring into your conversations self-validating statements that will cultivate a finer appreciation of your strengths, successes, and noteworthy performances. In overcoming the myth of modesty you provide yourself with the recognition you previously sought from others. When all and everyone else fails, you can always count on yourself!

- *Develop emotional and behavioral detachment.* Above all, when questioning the irrational belief system that led to your dependent state, push yourself to turn around and walk away from the dependent quicksand. Forcefully demonstrate to yourself the idea that, "Yes, I got along without you and your accommodations, advantages, and favoritism before I met you, and I can damn well get along without you now." Taking the first behavioral step may well begin the momentum required to sever that emotional umbilical cord.

To paraphrase George Bernard Shaw, "If you sacrifice yourself for those that you love, you will end up hating those for whom you have sacrificed." For the purposes of emotional dependency, "If you depend on those who are important to you, you will end up being afraid of and angry at those on whom you depend." Emotional dependency is a drag for both participants. The "depender" often makes himself feel alternately hurt, anxious, depressed, and angry, while the "dependee" feels put upon, frustrated, and resentful about the symbiotic stranglehold. Therefore, if your goal is to be more joyfully and peacefully accessible to those you care about or would like to care about, liberate yourself from this self-inflicted dependency and fly free of the fear and anger it produces.

Note. From *Think Straight! Feel Great! 21 Guides to Emotional Self-Control* by Bill Borcherdt, ACSW, Copyright 1989, Professional Resource Exchange, Inc., P.O. Box 15560, Sarasota, FL 34277-1560.

Do Not Forsake Me, Oh My Darling: Emotional Management in the Aftermath of Betrayal

Because betrayal frequently occurs suddenly and without warning, it abruptly disrupts what was previously expected from significant others. With virtually no time to prepare for this unexpected behavior from someone who is important to you, severe self-defeating emotional and behavioral reactions frequently occur. Whether from a mate, lover, child, friend, or work associate, betrayal is usually followed by a high level of emotional anguish and awkward, counterproductive behavior. Especially in love relationships, where one partner is ill-prepared for the rift in the relationship routine, the practical inconvenience is often intensified into an emotional holocaust.

This guide discusses sane, civilized responses to betrayal that limit emotions to grief and bereavement rather than letting them needlessly spill over into depression and hatred. When an important person severs mutually agreed upon exclusiveness and commitment, in lieu of committing suicide, murder, or other destruction, what can you do to lighten the emotional burden of experiencing a relationship whose foundation no longer exists?

The following suggestions are not intended to do away with unwanted feelings but instead to allow for better control of emotional responses to relationship adversity.

1. *Don't Assume the Inevitability of Disturbance.* Avoid the "self-fulfilling promise" of picturing yourself becoming emotionally unglued in light of the turnabout behavior of your important other. Understand that there are varied emotional and behavioral means that will allow you to avoid this pitfall. By brainstorming alternatives to despair and hatred, you will prepare yourself to keep an emotional lid on your response. Imagining yourself as not being at the mercy of your circumstance or environment will contribute to your emotional sanity by softening the blow that stems from taking uncertain and unpredictable conduct in others too seriously.

2. *Don't Personalize.* Keep in mind that although someone suddenly discriminates against you in violation of a previous understanding, in no way is your value to yourself diminished. This will frustrate and deprive you, but it need not humble you. Remind yourself that other people's opinions and behaviors toward you do not equal you. Hurt can be minimized by avoiding self-blame and self-pity. Depression and anger can occur only if you blame yourself or blame the other person. You can instead care less about the other's patronage without becoming uncaring.

3. *Attribute Fault to the Other.* Realize that the other's fickle behavior says a lot about him or her but very little about you. Perhaps this person lacks long-range staying power, is indecisive and wishy-washy by nature, lies with a straight face, has a low threshold for tolerance of the discomforts often found in a close relationship, or in other ways lacks the persistence required for more than temporary commitment.

4. *Identify New Opportunities.* Try to think of options that you wouldn't otherwise have had.

Sometimes he or she who travels alone travels faster and with a wider variety of other advantages. Being without an exclusive relationship commitment makes it more convenient to test out other vocational, educational, and relationship waters. Try to avoid the plight of Mark Twain's cat who, after being burned on a stove, avoided all stoves he came across. All stoves, relationships, and personal opportunities are not alike, so escalate your feelings of hope and appreciation for possible advantages you might discover by experimenting further.

5. *Look to the Future.* Project yourself into time and try and see that, months and years down the road, present discomfort will likely be a faded memory.

6. *Let Time Pass.* Accept the reality that you are not going to instantly feel better. Allow yourself the time required to emotionally heal from your misfortune.

7. *Stay Active.* Find constructive distractions that will permit the acceptance process to sink in. The more involved you become in life, the less you will get entangled in your unhappiness.

8. *Trust Yourself.* Follow your inclinations to do what you think is best for you. Avoid taking unsolicited, well-intended advice from friends, or psychological recipes in the form of "stages" the experts might say you must go through to bring closure to your grief. Respect your individuality and cherish the idea that no one knows what's best for you but you.

9. *No Report Card.* Avoid the human tendency to give yourself a bad report card either for doing a bad thing or for being in a bad situation. Judge and be disappointed in your circumstances, and whatever you may have done to get yourself into them (lest you make the same mistake in the future), but don't judge yourself. Instead, see that you are not on trial.

10. *No Double Whammy.* If you slip and wrongly get down on yourself, don't further magnify your disturbance by getting down on yourself

for getting down on yourself. No one handles difficulty perfectly well, so take a compassionate view of your self-inflicted disturbance rather than give yourself a problem about giving yourself a problem.

11. *Don't Condemn the Other.* Prevent yourself from bringing on unwanted rage and bitterness that make a chronic problem out of a temporary difficulty. If your goal is not to emotionally linger in your troubles, push yourself to accept the difficult reality that just as you have a right to be wrong, the other has an equal right to trespass important values.

12. *Avoid Self-Pity.* Try to accommodate the idea that life is full of surprises, and through problems you are likely to have learned some things about yourself. Earmarking these advantages may help to counter tendencies to wallow and remain mired in your self-pity.

13. *Destroy the Ego.* Don't make an ego problem out of your predicament. Understand your difficult circumstance to be a distinct disadvantage which makes you worse off, but not a worse person. Likewise, after you emotionally regroup you will be better off, but not a better person.

14. *See the Big Picture.* Be aware that although one part of your life has quickly deteriorated, your whole life doesn't have to go down the tubes. Instead, reinvest your time and energies in appreciating and benefiting from that part of your life over which you still have some control.

15. *Take a Noncommercialized View.* Question the not so subtle slants of the media's presentation of how to deal with betrayal. Although practically all those in media portrayal threaten to kill others or themselves in the face of betrayal, you are not required to take such a soap-opera stance. Instead, opt for a more civilized, healthier outlet that allows for more sensible, balanced emotional containment and expression.

110

Is it hard to do yourself a favor by not flipping your emotional wig in the aftermath of betrayal? A definite yes. Is it harder not to opt for self-control in the face of this same circumstance? An even more definite yes! The alternatives outlined in this guide go against social and media models and may require a philosophical overhaul of your ideas about what a significant other's violation of relationship codes means for you. Betrayal in a relationship that has had special meaning is far from most people's idea of a good time. Valuing and trusting yourself enough to think and act in ways that ward off emotional breakage is an elegant way to cultivate a fuller appreciation of yourself, even when someone else doesn't. If you can always find value to yourself, an adverse experience can, in the long-run, help you learn to be more self-accepting and emotionally self-sufficient.

Note. From *Think Straight! Feel Great! 21 Guides to Emotional Self-Control* by Bill Borcherdt, ACSW, Copyright 1989, Professional Resource Exchange, Inc., P.O. Box 15560, Sarasota, FL 34277-1560.

Marital Dissatisfaction Versus Marital Disturbance: Not Putting the Cart Before the Horse

If a marriage is to survive and thrive, "The art of being wise is knowing what to overlook." If not, conflict and boundary disputes arising from human imperfection and individual differences are likely to dominate an otherwise potentially harmonious relationship. Dissatisfaction occurs in marriage when one partner does something that the other doesn't like, or doesn't do something the other would like done. Disturbance results when an exaggerated meaning, and consequent reaction, is given to whatever isn't approved of. Dissatisfaction about a negative marital happening can be managed so as not to become a disturbance. Although most people in similar circumstances probably would make themselves angry, it is not necessarily the emotionally healthy thing to do.

With attitude skill training, partners can learn to remain rationally annoyed rather than making themselves irrationally angry, allowing them to solve problems in a more clearheaded, helpful manner. Yet a majority of marital improvement efforts focus almost exclusively on changing the presenting dissatisfying event, for example, negative criticisms, faulty communication patterns, and traits or features that don't suit one of the partners. Such behavioral-restructuring efforts are in error, and though well-intended and apparently effective in the short-run, in the long-run are inefficient and counterproductive. Though partners may temporarily feel better, they do not get better and may even get worse. This guide explains why this is so and puts forth a more comprehensive system of ideas that enables more long-standing results.

Marriages are not made in heaven, and therefore a degree of reasonable inequality exists in any marriage. Mates best accept this reality from the start. Falling-out in marriages frequently begins when one partner acts badly, for example, doesn't communicate or does so in a critical way. The other partner generally creates anger, and before long the relationship deteriorates as both partners raise the marital roof in self-defeating ways. Efforts to better navigate such a conflict typically focus on the sender's behavior by encouraging or admonishing the negative or noncommunicator to act more tactfully or kindly and to change the way he or she sends messages while neglecting the emotionally disturbed reaction of the receiver.

Teaching people to give each other a lot of tender loving care, appreciation, and validation is a positive goal of communication skills training, but relying mainly on this affirmative approach in relationship discussions *doesn't*: (a) do away with the idea that because something is good, it has to be gained, and it is intolerable when it isn't; (b) increase a person's low frustration tolerance when deprived of another's positive attention; (c) acknowledge or prepare partners to deal with the ordinary neglect that tends to dominate many relationships; or (d) distinguish between effective and efficient problem-solving skills.

Successfully teaching communication and other relationship skills can help deal more effectively with a particular problem, such as when one mate feels slighted by the other. However, such situational improvement is only the tip of the iceberg when contrasted to more profound philosophical changes that allow one to transform upsetting feel-

114

ings about this particular problem and also deal more efficiently with future marital misgivings. This is accomplished by modifying insistent demands for ongoing kind, fair, and just treatment; giving up the seemingly ultimate, though impossible, dream of marrying the perfect mate; teaching what to realistically expect from another human being; and generally learning how to control yourself in response to negative behavior from your mate. An honest analysis of marital interaction will show that, because of human failings, irritating and annoying behaviors tend to reappear on the relationship scene. Adequate preparation for these realities goes beyond situation-specific conflict resolution skills to more efficient, thorough attitudinal skill training geared toward minimizing and transforming the emotionally upsetting response to such inevitable differences.

Behavior changes are well and good, up to a point. However, no matter how well people are taught communication skills, at times they don't follow their lesson plan. Unless tolerance training is foremost - how to get oneself less upset in the face of marital adversity - those involved will get themselves disturbed all over again when the other partner communicates in disenchanting ways. In fact, relationships can deteriorate further *after* couples "learn how to communicate" if they use hidden messages such as: "Tell me what is on your mind, but say what I want to hear"; or "Be honest, but don't let the truth get in the way." It is far better to first get both partners to understand and accept a more tolerant view that attacks the disturbance itself. The angry, disturbed reaction will be diminished considerably if mates change their demanding outlook of "Be where I am all the time or you don't love me." They best see that love and total agreement don't go hand in hand - that giving people room to be the way they are makes them more likely to become the way you want them to be. Loved ones have a right to be wrong and to act badly in numerous human ways, and if one asks a question, it is best to be prepared to hear a disagreeable answer.

Once a more tolerant climate is established, marital partners will be better able to determine their relationship destiny. As members of the marital team train themselves to get less disturbed about disagreeable attitude and behavioral tidbits, they will be able to forge ahead in programming bigger and better things into their togetherness.

The moral of the story is *first* to stop yourself from becoming disturbed about dissatisfying aspects of your marriage by not making yourself angry, resentful, or counterattacking. This will give you some perspective and allow you, if you choose, to present your concerns to your mate in a sensible, forthright manner that emphasizes compromise instead of finger pointing. This helping, facilitating approach not only lessens the negative, disruptive stimuli in your marriage, but helps you to become a more tolerant, accepting, compassionate, forgiving human being who is capable of even greater fulfillment.

Note. From *Think Straight! Feel Great! 21 Guides to Emotional Self-Control* by Bill Borcherdt, ACSW, Copyright 1989, Professional Resource Exchange, Inc., P.O. Box 15560, Sarasota, FL 34277-1560.

Twenty-Four Ways to Bring Out the Best in Parents

Most children would like to know how to get along better with their parents. Yet, while parents have access to many sources of expert advice on childrearing, few resources are available to help children build bridges instead of walls between themselves and their folks. Parent-child relationships are often seen one-sidedly as parents affecting their children, but children also affect their parents. What follows is a series of guidelines that balance this slanted perception - to help children improve their home environment by bringing out the best in their everyday contacts with their parents. These suggested alternatives are designed to accomplish relationship building:

1. Really push yourself to accept that your parents, like all other human beings, have many faults, have many problems of their own, are limited, and are sometimes too involved in those same problems plus making a living to help you with your concerns.
2. Don't blame your parents for their shortcomings, blunders, and wrongdoings, as you

wish not to be blamed for your own limitations.

3. Remember that you're not the only child in the universe who is required to have perfectly sane, fair parents.

4. Don't personalize or be thin-skinned about your parents' criticisms of your behavior. Avoid feeling hurt by seeing that their yelling and lack of appreciation for some of your actions doesn't diminish you as a person.

5. Don't depend on your parents in order to feel good about and accept yourself. Understand that just as their negative comments don't make you a bad person, their praise for a job well done doesn't turn you into a good person. You may be better off because of their praise and worse off without it, because they are likely to provide you with certain advantages following their praise and disadvantages after their criticism. However, remind yourself that just as being better off does not make you a better person, finding yourself worse off does not lead to being a worse person.

6. Recognize that gaining your parents' love and approval is nice but not necessary, important but not all-important. If you fail to gain their validation, you do not have to keep failing for the rest of your life at all other important tasks.

7. When you try to communicate with your parents, be prepared to hear answers you might not want to hear.

8. Find areas of agreement and purposely raise them in conversation with your parents.

9. Establish in your mind what you have in common with your parents and focus upon these alliances of interest.

10. Admit that accepting your parents' wishes and values by agreeing with them even when you don't want to is often in *your* best interest, because such efforts at joining and accommodation are likely to get you more freedom and privileges.

11. Surprise your parents in a positive way by doing nice things for them without being asked and when they least expect it.
12. When you are in the wrong, openly admit your mistake and apologize for it while indicating that you plan to do better next time.
13. Share your friends, schoolwork, thoughts, and feelings with them. This also serves your best interest, because the more they know about you the more likely they are to trust you and to feel comfortable about extending you privileges and advantages.
14. Discover activities you really like to do that are good for you and put a large amount of energy into them, such as work, sports, or a hobby.
15. Tell your parents what you're proud of and like in them.
16. Tell your parents what you're proud of and like in yourself.
17. Make a special effort not only to listen to what your parents say, but tune into and become an echo of their feelings; whether they are angry, sad, or worried, let them know you understand their feelings.
18. Realize that the grass isn't always greener on the other side, and that no matter who your parents were, there would be advantages and disadvantages. You will appreciate them more if you think about negative traits of other parents and zero in on the positive traits of your own parents.
19. Don't make the common mistake of expecting parents to take on all the positive features of your friends' parents. Instead, view them as individuals.
20. Tell your friends about some of the things that you appreciate in your parents. This may strengthen some of the pleasant feelings you have about them, and what you say may get back to them, encouraging a more friendly relationship.

21. When your parents make demands of you, even when they are unfair and unrealistic, understand that their wrongdoing is really a vote of confidence in your ability. Although their good intentions may not be backed by the right methods, they are really trying to tell you that they think you can do good things with your life.

22. Understand and accept that sometimes your parents will error in expecting more of you than they expect of themselves. Because your parents do or don't do something doesn't justify your decision on the matter. As an individual, make choices that are well thought out and that you believe are in your present and future best interests. It does not follow that "well, you smoke," "you didn't go to college," "you lose your temper easy," "you got married young" reasons that you may give for your behavior are necessarily right for you just because your parents did them. Such ideas are many times a cop out to not put forth the effort required to do the best for yourself.

23. Consider ideas you hold that lead to emotional upset with your parents, and challenge your thinking. These mistaken notions often have to do with a demand put on yourself, your parents, or the quality of your relationship with them. Some ideas that lead to becoming upset are:

- "I should be more the way my parents want me to be, and I'm less of a person when I don't live up to their expectations of me";
- "My parents should not act the way that they frequently do, and they should be blamed and gotten angry at when they do";
- "Living with my parents should be a lot easier than it is; I can't stand it when things are tough."

Review and debate these three notions, changing them to:

- "I sometimes wish that I could behave more the way my parents want, and it is regrettable that I don't more often, but not being on the same wavelength as my parents does not diminish my value to myself as a human being";
- "Although I would like my parents to act differently than they sometimes do, they have a right to follow their own mind in choosing their own views and actions. Furthermore, when they wrongly follow their own way of thinking, it does no good to get myself angry at them and blame them for what I believe to be their errors in judgment";
- "I certainly wish that associating with my parents were a lot easier than it often is, but it doesn't help when I moan and complain about how awful their way of living is. I would make it easier on myself if I realized that it's not the end of the world when they don't see things my way."

Becoming less demanding of yourself, your parents, and your relationship with them can take a lot of pressure off all concerned, encouraging better things between you.

24. *Honestly* ask yourself why your parents bother to go through the time and effort to correct/discipline/supervise you. Is it because they hate your guts and wish to do you in, or don't have better things to do, or is it out of a genuine caring interest in how your life turns out?

These attitude and behavior possibilities will not guarantee better relationships with your parents. However, it is unlikely that you will bring out more harmony with them unless you consider and use at least some of them. If children, like parents, can better accept themselves and their significant others in spite of mutual faults and mistakes, and better accommodate and provide for the others' wishes, the chances of reaching their mutual goal of bringing out the best in the other while pulling off a happier living arrangement will be much greater.

Note. From *Think Straight! Feel Great! 21 Guides to Emotional Self-Control* by Bill Borcherdt, ACSW, Copyright 1989, Professional Resource Exchange, Inc., P.O. Box 15560, Sarasota, FL 34277-1560.

Doing the Right Thing
for the Right Reason:
Rational Assertiveness Training

Assertiveness may be defined as (a) the ability to express and take action on behalf of yourself without intentionally hurting others, (b) the capacity to respond in a way that is in your best interest, and (c) determinedly seeking what you want, while energetically and passionately refusing to accept what you don't want.

There are varying dimensions to such self-choosing verbal and behavioral expression, including:

- asking bold questions;
- making bold statements;
- clearly and forthrightly telling someone how you feel without telling them off;
- making "I" statements, for example, "I am concerned" rather than "You make me concerned";
- giving opinions;
- seeking out opinions;
- unashamedly admitting ignorance or lack of understanding on your part;
- active persuasion;
- expressively overcoming timidity, shyness, and social avoidance or withdrawal;
- making positive statements about your abilities;
- soliciting help with a problem you have;

- unapologetically saying no in refusing a request;
- making a request;
- refusing to answer a question;
- responding effectively to criticism;
- refusing to do things for others that they can best do for themselves;
- refusing to let others do for you what you do best for yourself;
- handling put downs;
- handling put offs;
- giving compliments; and
- receiving and accepting compliments.

Such examples of responsible self-expression can be implemented in varying ways for varying reasons. The significance of such expression is not just what you do, or how you do it (as in nonverbal communication such as eye contact, tone of voice, or body posture), but more comprehensively, the reasons *why* - the philosophies, convictions, goals, and intentions behind your efforts. My premise is that much of what is popularly considered to be assertiveness skill training is done for reasons that, however unknowingly, result in participants doing the right thing for the wrong reason. As a consequence they temporarily feel better, but in the long-run they get worse. Pernicious side effects of self-help expressional tools are frequently overlooked by trainers and consumers who wrongly assume that the ends justify the means, that effectiveness is equivalent to efficiency, and that a pragmatic approach to problem-solving assures no harm can be done.

In fine tuning such goal attainment, one finds many good intentions which, because they are not backed by the right methods, do injustice to recipients of such self-help services. Client expectations are heightened as they are led to believe that, because a specific behavioral skill is learned for effectively and pragmatically dealing with a difficult interpersonal situation, the problem is therefore solved. This is far from the truth. Helpers more often than not (a) assume that clients want to solve this problem rather than learn how to more comprehensively problem-solve, and (b) are not aware of, or do not subscribe to, a system of ideas that opts for gains within gains by allowing total rather than situation-specific problem-solving. So, if you are interested in more than a palliative, partial, temporary behavioral skill-training solution that may well do more harm than good, and instead prefer more complete, enlightened solutions to problems of daily living, this guide is for you!

Various forms of communication skill training generally, and assertiveness training specifically, become the devil in disguise in several ways. These faulty justifications and methods can be traced to two interconnected basic categories:

1. Cognitive laxness, or slippage includes efforts that result in behavior change without alteration in the philosophical views that created the emotional disturbance to begin with. Circumstantial changes may occur, but the emotional disturbance is not modified because the cognitive correlates of the disturbance, such as anger and anxiety, are not transformed. Because the base of the emotional upset goes unattended, the disturbance continues, possibly in aggravated form, the next time the individual is confronted with a similar problem situation.
2. Specific social and cultural values, meaning differing forms of conventional wisdom, may go unquestioned. In this category are a lust for success, defining performance as a valid indicator of personal worth, self-proving rather than self-accepting, a belief that certain conditions in life are intolerable, and worship of the cultural god called "ease." In fact, short-cut solutions that result in long-term difficulties are offered because it is immediately convenient for both the client and therapist, who are in cahoots to solve the presenting problems in a way that is easier in the short-run, but harder in the long-run.

The following are examples of short-sighted, and often counterproductive, yet assertive solutions:

1. The expression of anger or aggressiveness in an assertive, constructive way that gives the illusion that the problem is solved when in reality it may be just beginning. Some assertiveness trainers teach the expression of negative emotions in socially approved ways, but frequently leave the demanding, 2-year-old philosophies that created the resentment unattended. As a result, asserters feel better but get worse in that feelings of anger and hostility get practiced and reinforced by expression. Eventually, participants get themselves angry all over again as the intolerant philosophies continue to dominate. Assertive behavior by itself can lessen your potential to become a more tolerant, nonjudgmental human being. In fact, after getting rid of anger by challenging your condemning, intolerant views, you may well decide in a more clearheaded, sane, undisturbed fashion to *not* assert yourself, and instead to accept the annoying circumstances as they exist.

2. Feeling nervous or anxious may create discomfort about the feelings of anxiety themselves, and wrongly lead to the conclusion that "I have to do something in an assertive way to get rid of these uncomfortable feelings which are intolerable." Here again, your tolerance level takes a drop because you believe that certain uncomfortable feelings are unbearable and should therefore not exist. Such heightened demands for comfort feed into a more general human tendency toward low frustration tolerance - complaining and whining about the inevitable unpleasantries in life. For instance, if you are uncomfortable socially because you are telling yourself that "I should be saying more; it makes me feel anxious when I'm so quiet; I can't stand myself when I am acting or feeling

this way," you may assert yourself and to some degree feel better, but really not have worked on the core difficulty in accepting yourself as fallible and imperfect.

3. Disapproval anxiety refers to an individual's overconcern about what others might be thinking about him or her. Just as you can act morally for the right reason (from an enlightened desire to help members of your social group), or the wrong reason (because you fear what others might think of you if you don't), one can assert yourself for good, self-interested or bad, social-pressure reasons. Putting on the psychological cosmetics and acting like a plastic saint may *appear* to be the right thing to do, but may be done out of a self-conscious fear of disapproval and dislike from others. Examples of this approval-seeking trap are parents who discipline their children out of concern for what other parents present might think if they don't; a person who asserts himself or herself in the face of another's criticism, not so much out of a concern about the criticism itself but because others may think less of him or her if an assertive stand isn't taken; someone who says no to a companion only out of a fear of appearing weak; or one who deals assertively with a put down simply to avoid appearing ineffectual or incompetent. It may seem that such individuals are self-confident and are gaining, via assertion, better control over their lives. However, in reality they are feeling insecure and losing control, putting their emotional and behavioral prerogatives in the hands of how others may view and accept them for asserting or not asserting themselves.

4. Compulsively asserting yourself or assertively helping others does not lead to greater self-compassion or greater self-acceptance. Assertion motivated by guilt prevention is tied in with the perfectionistic, self-blaming belief that "I have to do the right thing at all times

and when I don't, I become diminished as a person and am of lesser value to myself."

5. Asserting oneself for ego, psychological one-upmanship reasons may feed an exalted self-image, but because this self-defined ego massage is based on false premises and assumptions, one's emotional well-being will eventually falter. Becoming a patron or connoisseur of assertion, and believing that your achievements generally and becoming assertive specifically makes you a better person, will result in the emotional flip-flopping that any conditional self-acceptance produces. You are not your assertiveness skills, and this form of one-upmanship will ultimately lead you down the garden path of one-downmanship.

When is it advisable, then, to assertively plant your own garden rather than wait for someone to bring you flowers? The following two basic guidelines will allow you to exercise your assertive option in a more clearheaded, well-thought-out manner:

1. Be preferentially motivated to assert yourself rather than demandingly insistent that you "have to." Be flexible and selective in choosing how, when, and where to express (or not express) yourself. Don't get locked into a rigid way of thinking that narrows your alternatives and blocks what could be wiser, more situationally appropriate (though unassertive) choices. Don't get trapped by frozen definitions that encourage you to parrot preconceived ideas of how certain tough interpersonal circumstances are to be dealt with. Having a working knowledge of assertiveness tools does not mean you have to use them.

2. Put your assertive foot forward only when it is to your advantage to do so, and not just for the sake of doing it. Often it is more profita-

ble in the long-run to live with frustrations on a temporary basis, and to get rid of anger, guilt, disapproval anxiety, discomfort anxiety, and ego problems *prior* to making a decisive choice, assertive or not. Clearheaded consideration of the matter may indicate that (a) it wouldn't be advisable in the present circumstances to follow assertive dogma, for example, in a marriage or on a job where assertively expressing yourself could escalate rather than remediate problems; (b) you may, because you have more tolerantly controlled your dissatisfaction level, not wish to spend the time and energy on a circumstance that you now view in a less significant way. In short, as you diminish, minimize, and control your self-created disturbances about these circumstances, they may no longer be a significant problem for you.

Assertiveness tools, methods, and techniques may or may not be the desirable alternative for you at any given point in time. After weighing the pros and cons of the choices available, make your ultimate decision in a forthright, unashamed, nonapologetic way. Do so within a philosophical frame of reference that allows you to avoid rigid and assertively addictive attitudes and promotes your higher frustration tolerance, breeds greater self- and other-accepting views, and does not perpetuate or conceal low frustration tolerance. Certain conditions of life are unpleasant, but this does not mean they are intolerable and unbearable. Condemning and demanding views that insist that others be just like you; self-flagellation if one has working knowledge of how to use something and intentionally or unintentionally doesn't; protecting oneself from others' disapproval by asserting oneself against unkind comments and criticisms rather than fully accepting oneself in spite of them, will all ultimately risk greater problems between you and your social group. Doing the right thing for the right reason may well, in the long-run, enable you to better influence and more harmoniously live with yourself and your associates.

Note. From *Think Straight! Feel Great! 21 Guides to Emotional Self-Control* by Bill Borcherdt, ACSW, Copyright 1989, Professional Resource Exchange, Inc., P.O. Box 15560, Sarasota, FL 34277-1560.

Avoidable, Nonaffordable Accompaniments of Depression

Depression, "the common cold of mental health," is often seen as a singular problem. However, there are many dimensions to depression called the secondary problem or symptom stress. One of the hallmarks of rational-emotive therapy (RET) is attacking this "reaction to the reaction" as a first step in the problem-solving process. Unless these other disturbances are dealt with initially as problems in and of themselves, layers of stress will accumulate, making it very difficult to resolve the primary identified depression. Additional upsets prevent the type of clear thinking best promoted to conquer the presenting difficulty, not only perpetuating, but amplifying and escalating the original symptom. Whether the initial, observable depression reaction stems directly from a biochemical imbalance (endogenous depression) or is a more direct reaction to situational stress (reactive depression), humans have a natural inclination to, as Mary Poppins once said, "Trouble trouble, and you will be troubled."

Depression is a handicap, but it does not have to be magnified into a disability. This guide identifies these additional emotional difficulties and addresses how they can effectively be overcome. Possible levels of depression, each of which is seen as a problem in its own right, include the following:

1. The seeming main or presenting depressed mood itself;
2. Depression about the depression when self-describing how terrible and hateful this problem is;
3. Feelings of guilt, which are an offshoot of self-downing and self-blame for having the negative trait of depression. In this sense, the depression takes on the additional proportion of an ego problem;
4. Feelings of shame and embarrassment because others have or may have discovered that you are presently emotionally down and may therefore think worse of you. Shame differs from guilt in that the issue is others' disapproval rather than self-disapproval;
5. Feeling sorry for oneself for being depressed while the rest of the world goes on its presumably merry way;
6. Fear and anxiety because of such emotionally charged notions as: "What if it gets worse?"; "What if it goes away but comes back?"; "What if I can't stand it?"; and other urgent, desperate self-sentences.

Any one of these often hidden secondary stresses can mushroom into a bigger problem than the primary recognizable disturbance, thus extending or even magnifying the original emotional discomfort. As long as the symptom of depression becomes a focal point for self-blame, fear, anxiety, guilt, shame, and self-pity, the primary depression can't run its course and fade away, which most depressions will do; instead, its detrimental influence is reinforced and expanded.

Depression is a tough problem! To manage its primary effects and avoid this double emotional jeopardy, this condition requires tough-minded attention. Remedial efforts include the standard operating procedures of RET - identifying, challenging, and uprooting irrational beliefs while taking forced, constructive action. Attacking accompanying discomfort, disapproval, and ego anxieties will help prevent aggravating what already exists. Accepting the problem while working against changing irrational ideas can contain and remove the disorder. Strongly asking yourself challenging questions like these will go a long way toward building a case for emotional self-control and self-acceptance:

1. "Granted that depression is no fun. But where is the evidence that it means my life has to be totally bleak, and why can't I stand this condition that I truly don't like?"
2. "Depression is a lousy deficiency, but why can't I accept myself in spite of it, and how does having this probably momentary trait make me a totally deficient person?"
3. "True, others may disapprove or make fun of me in some way if my problem becomes public knowledge, but why couldn't I tolerate that? Why is it anything to be ashamed of?"
4. "Others have problems too; they may not have the same difficulty I am having at this time, but nobody is perfect. Why must life be fair to me by providing me with emotional happiness, and why do I have to feel sorry for myself when it doesn't?"
5. "Granted, my condition could get worse, and if it does get better it might come back at a later date; but even so, why would that be intolerable? Why couldn't I again, and again, and again, if necessary, challenge myself to conquer it repeatedly?"

Use of these questioning hypotheses encourages you to do what is best for yourself whether you feel like it or not, which often leads to feeling like doing it after you get caught up in the spirit of the activity. If you wait until you feel like it before you do what is desirable, you may wait a lifetime and not get around to completing the action. Forced action permits you to engage in antidepressant, pleasuring, self-interested activities as a way to overcome your depression and its derivatives. Although overcoming depression and its frequent accompaniments is not easy, inaction will leave you with two or more problems of disturbance for the price of one.

Note. From *Think Straight! Feel Great! 21 Guides to Emotional Self-Control* by Bill Borcherdt, ACSW, Copyright 1989, Professional Resource Exchange, Inc., P.O. Box 15560, Sarasota, FL 34277-1560.

Where There's a Will There's a Won't: Twenty-One Not-So-Good Reasons to Put Off Until Tomorrow What Has Already Been Put Off Until Today

If changing present patterns of behavior is so beneficial in the long-run, why is such long-range productive action usually put on the back burner? This collection of guides addresses the human tendency to rationalize avoiding the long-term, profitable thing and justify doing the short-run, counterproductive thing, based on these three reasons:

1. *Genetic Tendencies Toward Lethargy and Inertia.* We don't teach people to procrastinate, yet stalling and dilly-dallying are so frequent that it would be logical to conclude the existence of an inborn predisposition to this problem. Whether it be personal maintenance tasks (term papers, household responsibility, projects of varying sorts), self-development goals (furthering education, developing a special interest, overcoming personal problems), or interpersonal aims (making a social contact, attempting to resolve a conflict with someone, or working at being on time), avoidance and inaction tend to run rampant.

2. *It's More Immediately Convenient to Self-Sabotage Over the Long Haul.* When a momentary decision is made to hold off rather than

to go ahead with constructive action, a rush of relief is experienced from knowing that energy and effort will be preserved, even though opportunities will be lost, relationships will become strained, general health/habits will continue to falter, and the general quality of life will lessen. Avoiding the wear and tear necessary to achieve a given goal seems like such a lustful, relaxed premium, despite the long-range handicap to one's convenience and fulfillment.

3. *Failure to Focus on the Ultimate Advantages and Benefits of Completing a Given Task, However Immediately Difficult to Do.* Until change is foreseen as bringing with it increased pleasure and personal gain, it is unlikely that the required motivation to accept present pain for future gain will be generated. In sizing up the pros and cons of involvement in a given activity, if the dominant contemplations are the short-run hassles, frustrations, deprivations, and inconveniences rather than the long-range fulfillments, discouragement and gloom will likely predominate. It is more motivating to keep in mind the ultimate healthful, personal efficiency, economic, and other gains that will accrue and focus in on these.

Here are 21 self-sentences, cognitive inventions, philosophic fictions, and internal creations frequently manufactured as justifications for procrastinating.

1. "It's *too* hard." This lazy-bones view and its derivatives are probably behind much of the sidetracking that occurs on the way to problem-solving and goal achievement. Best intentions are dashed when low frustration tolerance or discomfort anxiety sets in. The valid premise that something is difficult is turned into an illogical conclusion that it is "too hard," "shouldn't be that hard," or "I can't stand it" being so troublesome. These notions stall start-

ing momentum and leave one believing that the only alternative is being devastated by the awesomeness of the demands.

2. "I might fail - that would be awful and I couldn't stand that." Procrastination becomes an ego problem if fear of failure dominates. With this psychological one-downmanship procrastination represents ego anxiety and the fear of failure.

3. "I'll get even." Stalling, tardiness, or leaving unfinished projects that inconvenience others can become retaliation and an expression of resentment, anger, and hostility over past felt injustices. What is actually accomplished here is the proverbial cutting off one's nose to spite one's face.

4. "I'll do it later." Waiting for the tomorrows that never come is a typical rationalization. Talking about a task or problem is a poor substitute for doing something about the task at hand.

5. "I'll do it after I do something else." Although there is temporary relief in deciding to do something else less demanding first, the decision still skirts the main issue.

6. "But I don't really feel like doing it." The myth that one must feel like doing what is best, especially if it takes energy to accomplish it, assures sedentariness. Whether it is counting the number of angels on a pinhead, completing a monthly report on time, or doing some other laborious, loathsome task, it is better to get started on it. Engaging in "as-if" behavior by extending your energies even (especially) when not in the mood will frequently generate even more incentive.

7. "It's not like me." The idea that moving into virgin territory, however potentially to one's advantage, would be too far out of present character is related to (a) inherent bias against change, the unfamiliar, and the belief that because something is different it's bad; and (b) disapproval anxiety or an overconcern about

what others might think when they see you in this new light. To get tied up in emotional knots about possible lack of acceptance for your efforts will leave you stymied and mired in the status quo.

8. "Others might resist me or try to stop me." Conflict anxiety and the accompanying difficulties foreseen in managing others' passive or aggressive road blocks encourages taking a meeker route. The idea that one couldn't tolerate it if others would attempt to thwart and balk well-intended efforts is yet another encouragement to conclude that an undertaking is "difficult to do and therefore I can't do it."

9. "I shouldn't have to." This demanding, stubborn, rebellious dictate not only inhibits action, but also creates anger and resentment. Insisting that obstacles not exist when they do, and that energy expenditure not be necessary when it is, will prevent getting off one's duff and getting on with life.

10. "The time's not right." Waiting for the perfect time for the stage to be set prevents the show from getting started. Good intentions will not hold up under this insistence that at some magic moment in time all relevant factors will come together and spark a concerted (easy, of course) effort.

11. "I have to know for sure." The difficulty with living in a probabilistic world and the childish demands for certainty, surety, and orderliness show through here. Holding on to this infantile insistence on knowing tomorrow's answers today results in not getting the job done and reflects the self-statement that "I need a guarantee carved in granite that I am going to get an equitable return on my energy investment, and not having this gives me good reason for inaction."

12. "It's probably more trouble than it is worth." Without a crystal ball it's impossible to know what an end result might be, but this type of

sour grapes excuse puts off the requirements of a given project.

13. "Things aren't that bad the way they are now." This view promotes fence riding, lulling its believers into the complacent acceptance of what they have, however mediocre, and not wanting what they think is too hard to get.

14. "If I succeed, then what?" An often overlooked reason for getting off-track is the fear that if I succeed "I would have to continue to do so." Putting this type of pressure on oneself saps energy and discourages initial constructive action toward a given goal because "Having once succeeded, I wouldn't have any excuses for failing." Furthermore, "I would be forced to come face to face with my other problems." For example, finishing studying might bring one closer to the emptiness in one's life, or there might then be no excuse for avoiding new people or circumstances. In these ways, envisioned consequences of success can lead to heightened anxiety and avoidance.

15. "It's too scary." This fretful view about the horrors of putting oneself through a challenging experience discourages risk taking and a more experimenting, spirited, adventuresome view of life. It encourages hard-shell conservatism, fear of one's own shadow, and a frequent impulsive exit from the path that would more likely lead to long-run enjoyment and more effective living.

16. "What will other people think?" Fear of ridicule and scorn about public display of possible failings, shortcomings, and traits inhibits engaging in activities that are in one's long-run best interest. An example would be not exercising publicly in shorts because of stretch marks or darkened veins.

17. "I can't." This helpless, whining attitude excruciatingly self-describes the futility of any degree of effort. After all, if you can't do something you're beat before you start, so you

may as well not even think of rolling up your sleeves and going to work.

18. "If I'm going to do something I have to do it well, or I may as well not do it at all." This perfectionistic notion fails to recognize that much learning comes from the school of hard knocks, and that one will frequently go down many blind alleys before finding the way home. Things are seldom done well the first time, so if you wait until you can do something well before you do it, you may wait a lifetime.

19. "I might." "Maybe I will." "I probably will." "Yes, I'll do it, but . . . ." These qualifying, equivocating notions feed into a general human tendency to avoid the commitment required for change and retard personal development. Such investments pay low dividends in self-fulfillment and task accomplishment.

20. "I'm too busy (doing things for others)." Wearing fingers to the bone by trying to be all things to all people can result in diverting energy from one's own self-interest. Such self-sacrificial inclinations can be an all-too-convenient reason for not doing one's own difficult work.

21. "I have to know why I procrastinate before I cease this self-limiting, counterproductive activity." This belief that one has to study the problem before doing anything about it can result in curiosity becoming an end in itself and prevent the forced action required to achieve the desirable end.

Conquering the self-made resistances that go along with "a funny thing happened on the way to expected outcome" requires exploring philosophic alternatives while initiating forced action. Procrastinating tendencies are strong addictions that can be overcome by provable self-statements. Using the ABCs of Emotional Re-Education as invented by Albert Ellis, if at point A (activating event) you are faced with a difficult, yet important task

140

and at point C (emotional consequences) you feel lethargic and begin to dilly-dally, don't assume that the task itself or the difficulty of it is magically causing your emotional and behavioral inertia. Identify and examine what you are telling yourself at point B (beliefs). Chances are that you are telling yourself some of the 21 irrational ideas mentioned in this guide. Challenge these fictional ideas that you created at D (dispute, debate) in a concerted effort to beat your slothfulness and to passionately motivate yourself. If you diligently argue against your irrational notions and replace them with more sensible views, you will arrive at E (new effects), feeling more invigorated, energized, and less entrenched. You will act in a more long-term, self-interested way, and you will have a new belief system that allows you to look at difficult tasks more flexibly and motivatingly. By questioning your original assumptions about what failure, hard efforts, others' reactions, and short-run ease mean for you and by acting on your new, more progressive values, you can break away from those ideas that handicap your self-sufficiency, self-actualization, and personal development.

The table on pages 142 and 143 summarizes the earlier described 21 irrational beliefs and the alternative disputational beliefs.

TABLE 1: RATIONAL DEBATE

IRRATIONAL BELIEFS	DISPUTATIONAL BELIEFS
1. "It's too hard."	1. "It's difficult but not too difficult," "I wish it wasn't so hard but it is too bad that it is!" "Many of the things that are good for me are hard to do but not too hard or awfully hard."
2. "I might fail and that would be awful and I couldn't stand that."	2. "It's true I might fail, but failure isn't the worse of all possible crimes."
3. "I'll get even."	3. "Nonsense!" "If I try and get my pound of flesh I'll just hurt myself further and end up with bittersweet revenge."
4. "I'll do it later."	4. "I'd better do it now because I'll have other things to do later."
5. "I'll do it after I do something else."	5. "I'll do what is better for me to do now, even if it is more difficult to do than something else I can do later."
6. "But I don't really feel like doing it."	6. "I best do it anyway, once I get started on it my adrenalin will probably start to flow."
7. "It's not like me."	7. "Just because I haven't done it before doesn't mean that I can't start doing it now!"
8. "Others might resist me or try and stop me."	8. "Others have a right to try and discourage me, but I could tolerate that and press on."
9. "I shouldn't have to."	9. "Where is the universal law that I shouldn't have to go through the necessary steps to achieve a given result?"
10. "The times not right."	10. "There is no perfect time, the best time to try is now."
11. "I have to know for sure."	11. "Why do I have to demand to know tomorrow's answers today before I take that first step?"

142

IRRATIONAL BELIEFS	DISPUTATIONAL BELIEFS
12. "It's probably more trouble than it's worth."	12. "There may be some disadvantages but let me see if there would be just as many if not more benefits."
13. "Things aren't that bad."	13. "Things are going okay in many ways but maybe I can make them even better."
14. "If I succeed then what?"	14. "If I do succeed I wouldn't have to drive myself to keep succeeding if I didn't want to."
15. "It's too scary."	15. "There are some risks and chances involved but there is no gain without possible pain."
16. "What will other people think?"	16. "Others' opinion does not equal me."
17. "I can't."	17. "I won't know my potential until I try."
18. "If I am going to do something I have to do it well or I may as well not do it at all."	18. "Anything worth doing is worth doing poorly."
19. "I might," "Maybe I will," "I probably will," "Yes I'll do it, but . . . ."	19. "Knock off the horse shit and make a full fledged commitment.
20. "I'm too busy (doing things for others)."	20. "Better I rearrange my priorities and put myself first and others a close second rather than others first and myself a distant second."
21. "I have to know why I procrastinate before I stop doing so."	21. "Doing gets it done"; "Knowledge isn't the same as actions"; "It's not what you know but what you do with what you know."

Note. From *Think Straight! Feel Great! 21 Guides to Emotional Self-Control* by Bill Borcherdt, ACSW, Copyright 1989, Professional Resource Exchange, Inc., P.O. Box 15560, Sarasota, FL 34277-1560.

Marriage as Love and War:
To Love, Honor, and Negotiate

To increase the likelihood of love and decrease the likelihood of war, the first order of business in marriage is to focus on what goes right, taking more initiative to pleasure the other and not being so hard to please that you discourage well-intended initiative.

In *A Guide to a Successful Marriage* (1961), Albert Ellis asks and answers the question: "Is it possible to be sensible about marriage?" - "No, not really - but every little bit helps." This guide describes some behavioral and attitude skills that can help you to get more of what you want and less of what you don't want in marriage - more delight and less exhaustion, more joys and fewer hassles. One caution can be seen in a cartoon of a couple fighting by their front window; the wife is chasing her husband with a rolling pin in full view of another couple strolling down the sidewalk, who remark: "Say, isn't that our marriage counselor in there?" The moral of that story is that good advice is easier to give than to follow. Nevertheless, reasonable suggestions are presented here that, though hard to follow, may be even harder not to follow.

My four-step approach attempts to demystify the marital problem-solving process by replacing confusion, vagueness, and ambiguity with more precise, substantive tools and concepts that couples can use to sensibly carve out a more meaningful life together. Included are basic behavioral principles, assertion training, values realization, and fighting-fair concepts, all within the philosophical framework of rational-emotive therapy that says "Marital happenings don't disturb people - people disturb themselves about marital happenings." The four-step outline follows.

IDENTIFY INDIVIDUALLY
WHAT HAD BEST BE CHANGED

Marital change is a process of self- rather than other-analysis. No one has ever invented a way to change someone else; one can only change and be responsible for oneself. The more effective way to influence others, including mates, is to painstakingly and compassionately accept them the way they are, while taking the initiative to change your own behavior and/or attitudes towards their behavior and displeasing traits.

Acceptance and understanding have a way of building bridges instead of walls between people. People are more attracted to and influenced by those they believe understand them. Unlike the person who tries to talk you out of how you feel or believe, or who gives you a laundry list of reasons why you "shouldn't" feel or believe as you actually do, it is hard to argue with someone who accepts you without a set of expectations. Moving away from the self-defeating philosophies of "Be reasonable, do it my way," "Smile, dammit," and the 11th commandment - "My will be done" - toward a more accepting, tolerant view decreases conflict and increases the opportunities for marital harmony.

BEHAVIORAL CHANGES

1. Be selective in giving *negative criticism* by running negative commentaries through the six filters of criticism described by Sid Simon, a

pioneer in the values realization movement. A common question asked of a marriage counselor is: "What is the biggest problem in marriage?" My answer is the two-sided coin of negative criticism - giving too much of it and not receiving it very effectively, reflectively, and philosophically. Looking back on your own life you can probably count on one hand the number of times you were negatively criticized and your development was furthered because of it. Criticism that doesn't pass through the six filters described below is probably negative rather than constructive, and best left unsaid.

- Is the person in any shape to hear it? Take a mood sampling and determine if the timing is right. For instance, after a long hard day at work your mate would probably prefer talking about something other than his or her character defects.
- Are you willing to hang around and pick up the pieces? If your mate makes himself or herself upset by your comments, are you willing to stick around and play a supportive role rather than slam the door and walk out?
- Has your mate heard it before? If it has been addressed on many other occasions, it is best left unsaid because it will probably go in one ear and out the other, leaving you frustrated.
- Can he or she do anything about it? Be sure that the criticism is about something your partner is able to change, if desired.
- Is there any of your own material in it? Frequently we criticize others for features that we do not like about ourselves but tend to attribute to someone else.
- Would more validating help? Perhaps by responding more favorably and optimistically to your mate, you will encourage him or her to feel secure enough to look within and per-

haps change the very traits that you were directly attempting to modify.

2. *Deal with negative criticism* more effectively and less disturbingly. Marriages are not made in heaven. No matter how hard mates attempt to focus on their partner's strengths, slips will inevitably occur and faults and weaknesses will be emphasized. However, if you have the behavioral skills to more efficiently manage your response to criticism, conflict is less likely to snowball to unmanageable proportions. There are varying responses to criticism, and the truth is generally some place in between any two extremes. The tools listed below can assist in arriving at a more neutral emotional zone.

- *Reflective, attentive, or active listening.* When listening to people generally and when listening specifically to their negative criticism, it is better to respond less to the content and more to the feelings behind what they say. This approach sets a different tone and climate for the relationship by allowing each partner to maintain control of his or her response to the other's criticism while influencing the other person in a more positive way. It is hard to argue and fight with someone who understands how you feel; it is easy to argue and fight with someone who gives a list of reasons why you shouldn't feel that way or who angrily counterattacks. We tend to appreciate being understood at the feeling level, and this makes it more likely that we will, over time, take on the values of the person who is doing the understanding. The person who is criticizing is obviously unhappy and not at peace with himself or herself. To recognize this and to have a healthy sense of compassion in an actively understanding way promotes a no-lose type of interaction. Reflective listening also allows you to take a step back and to nicely refuse to either get upset about the person's problem or to believe that you have to find a solution to whatever the person is making himself or herself angry about. This also expresses your confidence in the other's ability to find his or her own solutions. Responding with "You sound angry," or "You seem really upset," is perhaps the most honest and obvious thing that can be said at that moment. Such understanding tends to take the wind out of the other person's sails, moderating intense feelings. Reflective listening also rewards people for their openness and encourages them to talk more freely in the future.

- *Fogging** is acknowledging the probability that there may be some truth to what is being said, while allowing you to remain your own judge of what you do. No matter what anyone says about you, there is always some truth to it, and reflecting back that truth will go a long way toward de-escalating conflict. It takes two ingredients to fight - an issue to fight about and two people who are willing to fight. Taking a step back rather than the typical two steps forward allows you not to be a part of the undesirable action. It is difficult to argue with or control someone who doesn't try to talk you out of how you feel and doesn't give you a list of reasons why you "shouldn't" feel the way you do. Thus, if a mate accuses a partner by stating "You are unfair," the spouse can throw up a fog and control his or her behavioral response to such criticism by partially agreeing, "Sometimes I do act unfairly."

- *Negative inquiry** means answering a question by asking one. Ask the person who is doing the criticizing a question about the criticism.

---

*Note. Terms appearing with an asterisk (*) are adapted from When I Say No, I Feel Guilty (pp. 323-324) by M. J. Smith, 1975, New York: Doubleday. Copyright © 1975 by Doubleday. Adapted by permission.

This allows you to control your response while making the other person accountable for being more precise. "Misery likes company," and when people criticize, it is because *they* are unhappy with themselves or their world in some way and want you to join them. These skills allow you to refuse that invitation, and by not giving that person an audience, the critical behavior is less likely to continue. Negative inquiry will influence the person to think twice before criticizing you again, remembering how you made him or her accountable for an earlier negative comment.

- *Negative assertion.** Strongly agreeing with the criticism if it is a valid one - for example, "That was a stupid mistake" - helps you deal with the belief that guilt is automatically associated with making a mistake, and that erring is the worst of all possible crimes.
- *Other possible responses* include "I am not sure - I want to think about it," saying nothing, simply agreeing, or saying, "I disagree."

3. *Learn Fighting-Fair Skills.* When people live together they are going to fight. Most of what people fight about isn't worth making into a major issue, and there are skills that can be used to contain such conflict. When you win by fighting unfairly, you lose by winning, inevitably hurting yourself, as well. The following ideas enable couples to agree to disagree fairly, openly, yet nondestructively.

- *Grave-digging.* Avoid fighting about the past, as this only opens up old wounds.
- *Finger-pointing.* Try not to make your mate out to be the bad guy and you the good guy. Instead, go into negotiations with the idea of creating solutions rather than blaming each other.
- *Mind-reading.* Check out your hunches about your mate, thus avoiding the illusory "marital

wave length." Don't expect your mate to read your mind. You would do better to ask for what you want.

- *Score-keeping.* Marriage isn't "50-50," it is more like 60-40, 70-30, or 80-20 depending on which day of the week it is. A certain amount of reasonable inequality goes on in any relationship, which is not a real problem unless individuals start to keep track of who is more right or who is more wrong, or who apologized last time.

- *Avoid giving back-handed compliments,* such as: "That dress looks very nice on you, dear - especially considering that you are 20 pounds heavier than the day that we got married"; or "You look real nice, dear - today."

- *Hitting below the belt.* After living with a person for awhile you know their vulnerabilities, things about which they typically upset themselves. Avoid this dirty-pool approach that can only escalate conflicts.

- *Stay away from the demand.* "Be where I am all the time or you don't love me." Love and total agreement do not go hand-in-hand. When you ask your mate a question, be prepared to hear an answer that you might not like. Avoid the "be sensible, do it my way" mentality. Give people room to be the way they are, and they are more likely to become more the way you want them to be.

ATTITUDE CHANGES

We frequently teach people how to respond to us by how we respond to them. As we retrain ourselves to deal more effectively with them, we reteach them some things about us. For instance, if you noticeably upset yourself about your mate's negative comment, obnoxious habit, or other unloving treatment of you, he or she is likely to engage more frequently in such unpleasantries. When people live together they sometimes unknowingly attempt to control each other, so if you give your mate an audience, a payoff, a reinforcer, such antics will be used again in the future: you are teaching your partner what it takes to get your attention, however negative. By not responding in a disturbed way, you create more tolerance, acceptance, compassion, and forgiveness. Once this type of atmosphere is established, you can more easily program bigger and better things into the marriage. "The art of being wise is knowing what to overlook"; simply keeping one's mouth shut in the face of verbal harshness is usually the better philosophy. The more you get yourself upset about your partner's upsets, the longer it takes for him or her to emotionally settle down. Also, the less you get yourself upset, the sooner your mate will be able to face and control his or her exaggerated feelings.

A common error made in marital negotiations is to opt primarily, if not exclusively, for behavioral restructuring. However, unless one learns to apply the principles of clear thinking to intimate relationships, such restructuring will not solve basic marital problems. Until mates learn to uproot some of their irrational ideas and demands about their spouse, themselves, and the institution of marriage itself, they may experience temporary relationship gains, but in the long-run will continue to undermine themselves because of unrealistic expectations. We are still in a self-help era, and there are many interpersonal effectiveness skills available to the interested customer. However, the underlying thesis of the rational-emotive approach to marital betterment is that in addition to behavioral skills designed to make things right, people primarily can use information on how to get themselves less upset when things go wrong.

In life generally, and in marriage specifically, every problem doesn't have a perfect solution, and behind every storm cloud there isn't a silver lining. Happiness is a direct ratio between what you expect and what you get. What is generally expected by individual marital partners is a mate who is an extension of them, who will cater to and totally agree with them, and who will completely live up to their expectations - not a separate entity with opinions, wishes, and preferences of his or her own. Beyond the mirages of marriage, one finds an imperfect human being who has wishes and expectations and characteristics and traits that may not be your marital cup of tea, and who is almost if not equally as fallible as you. To maximize fulfillment and minimize frustration, it is essential to give up this impossible dream of marrying a perfectly devoted, totally agreeing, and forever loving, forgiving, and caring mate. To increase one's tolerance level and get by this difficult roadblock, it is necessary to learn to expect and accept a certain amount of relationship incompatibility. To accomplish this, partners had best train themselves to give up these commonly held self-defeating marital notions:

1. I should become quite upset about my partner's problems and disturbances.
2. After my partner makes improvements in his or her attitude/behavior, I will follow suit and correct my part in the plot.
3. If my partner truly loves me, he or she will not differ in opinion or refuse my request but will go along with my ideas so as not to rock the boat.
4. Our past marital failures must have a strong, indefinite influence on how we can continue to get along.
5. My partner should act and think the way I would like him or her to, and I have no control over not being able to tolerate it when he or she doesn't.
6. I have to have my partner's love and approval all the time.
7. To prove my worth to my partner, I must be thoroughly confident, adequate, and achieving in all possible respects.
8. I should be able to perform sexually in a way that pleases my partner, and he or she must do the same for me.

9. When we disagree, I have to prove my point and disprove his or hers even if it means reviving unpleasantries.
10. My partner should notice my good points and positive efforts more often than he or she does.
11. My spouse deserves to be severely criticized/blamed/condemned when he or she makes a mistake.
12. When I make a mistake, admit I am wrong, or apologize, I am a weakling.
13. When my partner criticizes or condemns me, I can't stand it, and I have to counterattack.
14. There is invariably a right, precise, and perfect solution to all our problems, and it is catastrophic if this perfect solution is not found.
15. Trusting my partner is dangerous or fearsome. I should be terribly concerned about it and should keep dwelling on the worst that could occur.

Using the ABCs of emotional re-education as a learning tool, partners can self-master the means to not upset or disturb themselves during marital conflicts, frustrations, and deprivations. For instance, at point A (activating event) a spouse is criticized strongly for goofing in some way. Frequently, at point C (the emotional consequences) the receiver will feel angry about the sender's verbal barrages and wrongly believe that A caused C; for example, "He got me angry." Between A and C is B (belief about, interpretation of, self-talk about A), and it is these ideas that are creating the unwanted emotions of anger. These include such notions as: (a) "He shouldn't talk to me that way," "He has no right," and so on; (b) "It is awful, terrible, and horrible"; (c) "I can't stand it when he talks to me that way"; (d) "He stinks - what a global louse he is because of his uncalled for, lousy antics." In this way a case is easily built for instant emotional upset and condemnation. Self-control, acceptance (though not liking) of the other's behavior, and forgiveness of one's mate can best be achieved by instead moving to D (debate, dispute, self-argumentation, challenging) of the B's listed above by self-stating provable hypothesis such as: (a) "He has a right to speak his mind, even though I may wish that he wouldn't exercise his right." (b) "It is unpleasant and annoying, but certainly not dreadful, or the end of the world." (c) "I may have to bite the bullet, but I am a living example that I can stand it - because I can stand anything as long as I am alive." (d) "My partner may be committing a dreary act, but this doesn't make him a stinker to be condemned and counterattacked. This will only fuel the fire, influence him to feel worse about himself, and contribute to more mutual hurt."

The benefits of *forcefully and actively* disputing this matter will be: (a) arrival at the final step, E (new effects), at which an updated, more sensible, tolerant philosophy allows the receiver of the criticism to feel less upset in the face of annoying criticism from his or her partner, and to develop over time a degree of immunity to such unpleasantries; (b) creation of a more tolerant perspective and emotional climate that increases the probability of creating solutions rather than perpetuating domestic problems, thus breaking the cycle of negative behaviors and responses.

Now that we have identified individually what best be changed, the final three steps of marital negotiations follow.

DO IT! NO IFS, ANDS, OR BUTS

Move away from "shouldism" and "aboutism," where you talk and talk about the problems but don't do anything about them. Go to bat for yourself and your marriage even if you don't feel like it, and you may become absorbed in the spirit of negotiations. There is something motivating about standing behind yourself when working on your problems.

MAKE IT A POINT TO
NOTICE ONE ANOTHER'S EFFORTS

Positive behavior that goes unnoticed is less likely to recur. Once we teach other people what it takes to get our attention, we best reinforce that initiative and show appreciation for efforts if we want the positive changes to continue. Reach out to acknowledge positive efforts.

ACCEPT NEW WAYS OF
THINKING AND COMMUNICATING

This final step is harder than it sounds. When people have been thinking of their marriage as negative and failing, they frequently have a difficult time seeing it differently. This is reflected by statements such as: "This isn't like us"; "It feels strange"; "It will never last." Instead, it is important to reinforce your efforts by saying: "That is more like it"; "Let's have more of the same."

There are things you can *start* doing and things you can *stop* doing that will make a difference in your marriage. By keeping an attitudinal and behavioral lid on your own responses, you can experience fewer difficulties and differences. Stop trying to convince your spouse that you are right and he or she is wrong. If you put more effort into monitoring yourself, you will build a more meaningful relationship together. Marriage can be a joyful challenge or a painful test of endurance: the choice is yours. "Is it possible to be sensible about marriage . . . Sometimes, in some ways it is."

Note. From *Think Straight! Feel Great! 21 Guides to Emotional Self-Control* by Bill Borcherdt, ACSW, Copyright 1989, Professional Resource Exchange, Inc., P.O. Box 15560, Sarasota, FL 34277-1560.

Concerned But Not Consumed,
Involved But Not Entangled:
Avoiding Other Pity

This guide spells out the difference between encouraging independence, emotional self-sufficiency, and problem-solving capacities in another, as opposed to dependency, emotional babying, and stifling. The statement, "If you give a person a fish he will not starve today, but if you teach him how to fish he will be able to feed himself for a lifetime" illustrates the types of ideas, feelings, and actions that this guide promotes.

Particularly in relationships with significant others, people tend to get caught up in the rescuing process. "Rescuing" or "enabling" is when you try to do things for others that only they can do for themselves, such as trying to make others happy and getting them to "see the light" by accepting values and ideas that you know are in their long-run best interest. Examples include: (a) a parent who painstakingly attempts to make an academically disinclined child realize the importance of studying; (b) a friend or mate who forcefully tries to make his or her loved one less upset about one of life's grim realities, and gives a list of reasons why the other "shouldn't" be sad or disappointed; (c) a family member who makes continued persuasive efforts to get another to give up an addiction such as drinking or smoking; and (d) a parent with a mentally ill child who attempts to get him or her to renounce his or her psychosis.

Embarking on such helping projects, however well-intended, is doomed to failure, frustration, and mutual resentment. No one has ever invented a sure-fire way to change someone else, and it is highly doubtful that you as a rescuer will be the first. Beginning such a "mission impossible" is termed "head bashing"; you know before you do it that it is not going to work, but you attempt it in spite of the personal anguish that follows. It is commonly believed that if you do not try these other-saving efforts, you (a) are disloyal, (b) love the other person less, and (c) are less of a noble person for not persisting in assuming responsibility for another human's happiness and well-being. Good rescuing intentions chronically not backed by the right methods are frequently an attempt to evade the guilt and self-downing that follow from believing these false premises.

This other-rescuing triangle pitfall developed by Karpman has three points (see Figure 1, p. 159). Its process or communication chain is as follows:

1. The Rescuer (R) role begins with one person trying to save another from himself or herself. Such attempts fall on deaf ears; no matter what the rescuer or helper says, it is not what the person with the problem wants to hear. Frequently the person with the problems doesn't really want to change (though he or she may want different results), or wants to change what has already happened, which is equivalent to wishing for the moon.
2. As the Victim (V), the helper begins to feel unappreciated. All of his or her good advice is going for naught as the associate still doesn't change. The helper then begins to make himself or herself feel unappreciated, because in spite of his or her logic, reason, and words of wisdom, the other party still does not clean up

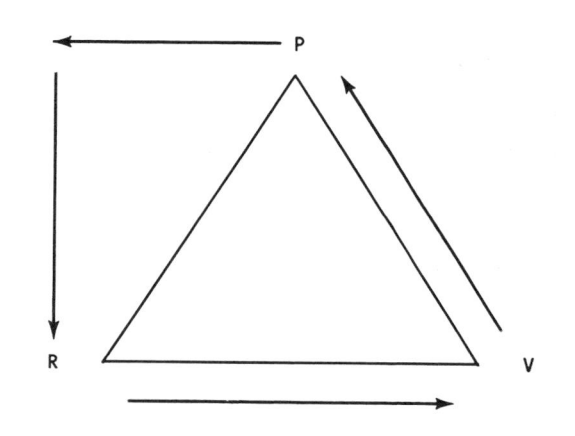

Figure 1. Other-Rescuing Triangle.

his or her act by changing self-defeating behaviors.

3. The Persecutor (P) role arises when the helper as amateur social worker makes himself or herself angry and flies off the handle, for very little apparent reason. Resentment over the loved one's lack of response surfaces, often in an angry, openly bitter fashion. At this same point, there is often a great deal of emotional fallout in the form of guilt, shame, and embarrassment for making oneself so angry at somebody who is loved so much. In an effort to atone for guilt feelings, the inclination is to go right back to rescuing, thus repeating this counterproductive style. Many people recognize that they are caught up in this vicious, spiraling cycle of encouraging helplessness, dependency, and mutual resentment, but don't

know how to get out of it. To learn how, read on!

Moving out of this relationship dilemma necessitates taking a step backward rather than two steps forward. This can be done by rethinking and changing one's attitudes and behaviors in this emotionally smothering and behaviorally strangling situation. The following two changes are required:

1. The first change requires adopting the idea that "I am not responsible for others' problems and disturbances; because I understand and accept this reality does not mean I love them less." In fact, by not trying to save others from themselves, you offer a vote of confidence by giving the message that "I am not going to try and save you from yourself, view you as an emotional cripple, or treat you with kid gloves because I believe you are capable and competent to figure out and act upon your own solutions to your problems." Instead of giving a laundry list of your own sensible answers to others' problems, prompt them to use their own reasoning and problem-solving abilities. Ask, "What is your plan?" If they have such a problem-solving map, suggest they test it out. If they don't have a plan, suggest they think of one and get back to you *after* deciding upon some new alternatives. This relieves you of the burden of other people's problems while encouraging autonomous thought, commitment, and effort. The results of these changes are a different definition of caring that will sensibly prevent you from getting trapped in your own former views of what concern and involvement mean. Media propaganda has encouraged the belief that happiness is externally caused, and the more upset you get about others' problems, the more you love them. Moving away from such arbitrary constraints to a more practical, productive view of caring is better for all concerned.

2. The second modification essential to escaping the ill-fated rescuing plight has to do with the way you listen to the other person's sadness, regret, and misfortune. People tend to listen to the content of what others say rather than the process or the feelings behind what is said. The capacity for and the skill required to empathetically tune into this feeling level has many advantages and is called reflective, attentive, or active listening. Using this technique enables you to compassionately respond to the other person's emotions about his or her problems, rather than creating your own unwanted feelings about his or her fate. It is helpful to be aware of a cardinal rule of human behavior: "misery likes company." If one person in a family, friendship, or social group is unhappy, the tendency is to want to share that misery with someone else. You can choose not to become "companions in misery" by simply stating: "You sound angry at your boss"; "You seem upset about your child's report card"; "It sounds like you are a bit afraid of going to school for the first time"; or "You seem concerned about your health." Keep in mind the importance of not saying anything else because it likely won't be what the other person wants to hear. Until you train yourself not to make yourself upset about others' problems, you will not be able to think very clearly, and as a result may use reflective listening less efficiently.

The following advantages result from combining this attitude and behavior change:

1. You reward people for their openness. By responding to their behind-the-scenes feelings, you encourage them to be more transparent with you in the future.
2. By not attempting to save the other person from himself or herself, you maintain control

of yourself while modeling for the other the advantages of not upsetting oneself.

3. This more tolerant, accepting, relaxed emotional climate has a soothing effect that also increases the likelihood of creating more precise, workable solutions.

4. Genuine understanding tends to elicit gratitude and appreciation while allowing more influence by the person who is openly demonstrating the understanding. The best way to influence someone is not by telling them how they should act, think, or feel, but rather to accept them the way they are. This listening skill, with practice, allows you to build bridges instead of walls.

5. The more deliberate you are, the better chance you have of helping. When you act acceptingly, reasonably, and understandingly you remove the other person's excuse for irrationality while maintaining control of your own faculties. Unable to entangle you in his or her problems, the other may eventually tire of shadow boxing with his or her own disturbances and begin to take more responsibility for his or her life.

Note. From *Think Straight! Feel Great! 21 Guides to Emotional Self-Control* by Bill Borcherdt, ACSW, Copyright 1989, Professional Resource Exchange, Inc., P.O. Box 15560, Sarasota, FL 34277-1560.

Bibliography

Alberti, R. E., & Emmons, M. L. (1975). *Stand Up, Speak Out, Talk Back!* New York: Pocket Books.

Alberti, R. E., & Emmons, M. L. (1982). *Your Perfect Right.* San Luis Obispo, CA: Impact.

Bach, G. R., & Wyden, P. (1968). *The Intimate Enemy.* New York: Avon.

Becker, W. C. (1971). *Parents Are Teachers.* Champaign, IL: Research Press.

Bell, N. W., & Vogel, E. F. (1965). *The Family.* New York: The Free Press.

Buntman, P. H. (1979). *How to Live with Your Teen-Ager.* Pasadena, CA: The Birch Tree Press.

Dobson, J. (1970). *Dare to Discipline.* New York: Bantam Books.

Ellis, A. (1961). *A Guide to a Successful Marriage.* N. Hollywood, CA: Wilshire Book Company.

Ellis, A. (1965). *Suppressed: 7 Key Essays Publishers Dared Not Print.* Chicago, IL: New Classics House.

Ellis, A. (1966a). *The Art and Science of Love.* Secaucus, NJ: Lyle Stuart.

Ellis, A. (1966b). *How to Raise an Emotionally Healthy, Happy Child.* N. Hollywood, CA: Wilshire Book Company.

Ellis, A. (1971). *Growth Through Reason*. N. Hollywood, CA: Wilshire Book Company.

Ellis, A. (1972a). *The Civilized Couples Guide to Extra-Marital Affairs*. New York: Peter H. Wyden, Inc.

Ellis, A. (1972b). *The Sensuous Person: Critique and Corrections*. Secaucus, NJ: Lyle Stuart.

Ellis, A. (1974). *Humanistic Psychotherapy*. New York: McGraw-Hill Book Company.

Ellis, A. (1975a). *How to Live with a Neurotic at Home and Work*. New York: Crown Publishers, Inc.

Ellis, A. (1975b). *A New Guide to Rational Living*. N. Hollywood, CA: Wilshire Book Company.

Ellis, A. (1979a). *The Intelligent Woman's Guide to Dating and Mating*. Secaucus, NJ: Lyle Stuart.

Ellis, A. (1979b). *Overcoming Procrastination*. New York: Signet.

Ellis, A. (1979c). *Reason and Emotion in Psychotherapy*. Secaucus, NJ: The Citadel Press.

Ellis, A. (1982). *Rational Assertiveness Training* (Audiotape). New York: Institute for Rational Living.

Ellis, A. (1988). *How to Stubbornly Refuse to Make Yourself Miserable About Anything--Yes, Anything!*. Secaucus, NJ: Lyle Stuart.

Ellis, A., & Abrahms, E. (1978). *Brief Psychotherapy in Medical and Health Practice*. New York: Springer Publishing Company.

Ellis, A., & Becker, I. (1982). *A Guide to Personal Happiness*. N. Hollywood, CA: Wilshire Book Company.

Ellis, A., & Whiteley, J. (1979). *Theoretical and Empirical Foundation of Rational-Emotive Therapy*. Monterey, CA: Brooks/Cole Publishing Company.

Fensterheim, H., & Baer, J. (1977). *Don't Say Yes When You Want to Say No*. New York: Dell Publishing Company.

Fraiberg, S. H. (1959). *The Magic Years*. New York: Charles Scribner's Sons.

Frankl, V. E. (1959). *Man's Search for Meaning*. New York: Touchstone Books.

Garcia, E. (1979). *Developing Emotional Muscle.* Atlanta: Author.

Garner, A. (1981). *Conversationally Speaking.* New York: McGraw-Hill Book Company.

Glasser, W. (1975). *Reality Therapy.* New York: Harper Colophon Books.

Greenberg, D. (1966). *How to Make Yourself Miserable.* New York: Random House.

Grossack, M. (1976). *Love, Sex, and Self-Fulfillment.* New York: Signet.

Haley, J., & Hoffman, L. (1967). *Techniques of Family Therapy.* New York: Basic Books, Inc.

Hauck, P. (1971). *Marriage Is a Loving Business.* Philadelphia, PA: The Westminster Press.

Hauck, P. (1974). *Overcoming Frustration and Anger.* Philadelphia, PA: The Westminster Press.

Hauck, P. (1976). *How to Do What You Want to Do.* Philadelphia, PA: The Westminster Press.

Hauck, P. (1978). *Overcoming Depression.* Philadelphia, PA: The Westminster Press.

Hauck, P. (1981). *Overcoming Jealousy and Possessiveness.* Philadelphia, PA: The Westminster Press.

Hauck, P. (1984). *The Three Faces of Love.* Philadelphia, PA: The Westminster Press.

Hoffer, E. (1966). *The True Believer.* New York: Perennial Library.

Holt, J. (1970a). *How Children Fail.* New York: Dell.

Holt, J. (1970b). *How Children Learn.* New York: Dell.

James, M., & Jongeward, D. (1973). *Born to Win.* Reading, PA: Addison-Wesley Publishing Company.

Johnson, W. R. (1981). *So Desperate the Fight.* New York: Institute for Rational Living.

Jourard, S. (1971). *The Transparent Self.* New York: D. Van Nostrand Company.

Lazarus, A. A. (1981). *The Practice of Multi-Modal Therapy.* New York: McGraw-Hill Book Company.

Lazarus, A., & Fay, A. (1975). *I Can if I Want to.* New York: Warner Books.

Maultsby, M. (1975). *Help Yourself to Happiness.* New York: Institute for Rational Living.

Paris, C., & Casey, B. (1979). *Project: You, a Manual of Rational Assertiveness Training.* Portland, OR: Bridges Press.

Paterson, G. R. (1978). *Families.* Champaign, IL: Research Press.

Perls, F. S. (1969). *In and Out of the Garbage Pail.* New York: Bantam Books.

Putney, S., & Putney, G. J. (1966). *The Adjusted American: Normal Neuroses in the Individual and Society.* New York: Harper Colophon Books.

Russell, B. (1971). *The Conquest of Happiness.* New York: Liveright.

Russianoff, P. (1983). *Why Do I Think I'm Nothing Without a Man?* New York: Bantam Books.

Satir, V. (1967). *Conjoint Family Therapy.* Palo Alto, CA: Science and Behavior Books, Inc.

Satir, V. (1972). *Peoplemaking.* Palo Alto, CA: Science and Behavior Books, Inc.

Shedd, C. W. (1978). *Smart Dads I Know.* New York: Avon.

Simon, S. B. (1978). *Negative Criticism and What You Can Do About It.* Niles, IL: Argus Communications.

Smith, M. J. (1975). *When I Say No, I Feel Guilty.* New York: Bantam Books.

Walen, S. R., DiGuiseppe, R., & Wessler, R. L. (1980). *A Practitioner's Guide to Rational-Emotive Therapy.* New York: Oxford University Press.

Weeks, C. (1981). *Simple, Effective Treatment of Agoraphobia.* New York: Bantam Books.

Zilbergeld, B. (1978). *Male Sexuality.* Boston, MA: Little, Brown, and Company.

Zilbergeld, B. (1983). *The Shrinking of America: Myths of Psychological Change.* Boston, MA: Little, Brown, and Company.

If you found this book useful...

You might want to read Bill Borcherdt's other book, *You Can Control Your Feelings! 24 Guides to Emotional Well-Being.* It is available for $19.70 per copy (includes shipping) from:

Professional Resource Press
P.O. Box 15560
Sarasota, FL 34277-1560

Telephone # 813-366-7913
FAX # 813-366-7971

All orders must be prepaid. Please send check, money order, or credit card number and expiration date (Visa, MasterCard, Discover, American Express accepted).

*   *   *

For a complete listing of all of our publications, please write, call, or fax the following information to the address and phone number listed above:

Name:_____

Address:_____

Address:_____

City/State/Zip:_____

Telephone:_____

Profession (check all that apply):

_____ Not in Mental Health Field	_____ Clinical Social Worker
_____ Psychologist	_____ Mental Health Counselor
_____ Marriage and Family Therapist	_____ Psychiatrist
_____ School Psychologist	_____ Other:_____